Photo by   Adamson & Son, Rothesay

JAMES COATES

[Frontispiece

Self-Reliance

Practical Studies in Personal Magnetism, Will-Power and Success, through Self-Help, or Auto-Suggestion

By

James Coates, Ph.D., F.A.S.

Author of
" Human Magnetism," "Seeing the Invisible,"
"The Practical Hypnotist," etc.

WITH ONE PLATE

LONDON
L. N. FOWLER & CO.
7 IMPERIAL ARCADE, LUDGATE CIRCUS, E.C.

NEW YORK
FOWLER & WELLS CO.
24 EAST TWENTY-SECOND STREET

1907

To all men who are in a rut,
 and want to get out ;
To all who are not afraid of work,
 and desire to turn it to the best advantage ;
To those who lack concentration,
 and drift without purpose ;
To all who lack success,
 and mean to have it ;
To the man who wants to know himself,
 and the man who thinks he does ;
And to all who desire to make
 LIFE WORTH LIVING,
This volume is earnestly and sincerely
 DEDICATED

Preface

HAVING some reputation as a Hypnotist and an expert student of human nature, I have been written to by many persons for advice and help. Very few of these correspondents have seen or are likely to see me in the flesh. Some of them have been hindered in life by some weakness, habit, or personal difficulty which they had failed to master, and which they—correctly or otherwise—believed hypnotism would remedy. In many cases, however, that was just the kind of help which they could not procure. No reliable operator—medical or lay—could be obtained in the part of the world where they resided. The outlook in many instances appeared to be black. And such have asked—" Can anything be done ?" "Can you help me ?" "Can I be cured ?—I feel that life is not worth living."

From the United States of America, Australia, New Zealand, India, Persia, Cape Colony, Natal, The Transvaal; from the Zambesia, the wilds of Rhodesia, the sun-baked lands of the West Indies; from homes in England, Scotland, and the evergreen fields of Ireland, correspondents appealed for help. As I believe in myself, and in the virtue of Self-Help, I advised them how to regard their difficulties, and told them how to CURE THEMSELVES.

The labour of writing innumerable letters had to be replaced by a uniform course of type-written lessons, in which the achievement of Self-Reliance was the leading theme. Being thoroughly conscious of the constitutional and cerebral differences in modes of thought and in character of those who wrote to me, the lessons were, when necessary, supplemented by suitable suggestions. The aim sought in both the lessons and the correspondence—whatever the position, education, special profession or trade of the correspondent—was to make the workman the better man, and the man the better workman ; to wish him to be satisfied with nothing less than the best in himself and in his work.

Self-reliant men are respected, believed in ; if opposed, can fight or defend. They are able to ignore the pin-pricks and the trials which upset others. They are able with prethoughtful purpose to overcome opposition, to attract what they desire, friends, affluence and success, while the men lacking Self-Reliance, without *grit*—the " miserable sinner, and worm of the earth " kind, who " are down on their luck "—lack the respect and the confidence of their fellows. Expecting to be ill, they are sick : feeling that there is no use in doing anything, they are idle ; expecting to fail, they fail ; expecting to be kicked, they are kicked—when some mean bully gets the chance. Both the self-reliant and the unreliant get what they have believed in and have—

consciously or unconsciously—sought. " Self-confidence
and some degree of push are absolutely necessary for
preservation. There is nothing truer than the value
men and women put on themselves is the value of the
world ; whatever less, never more."

While teaching my clients to believe in and trust
themselves (although the subject bristles with all the
profundities of health, vigour, and well-being of the
physical organisation ; cerebral psychology ; discrete
degrees of consciousness ; the conscious and the subconscious mind, and the " Double within us, which is
wiser than we " ; the voluntary and involuntary
machinery for the manifestation of Self, in which we
trust), I have avoided all technicalities and have
contented myself with merely pointing out those things
which are best to do, in order to create and develop
that trust. The lessons taught in this way have
brought letters of rejoicing from those who had the
faith and the patience to adopt the procedure suggested,
and who are to-day enjoying greater physical health, and
greater personal Self-control, success, and happiness, than
either experienced or even thought possible in the past.

As this volume has been produced in this fashion, a
strong, personal, friendly note runs through it ; from its
nature there is something of repetition, and no apology
is offered for either these or for the egotistical, optimistic
style in which it is written. And I am satisfied that
no one can read it *and carry out its suggestions* without
being stronger, brighter, happier, and more successful
in consequence. And happy is the man—while availing

PREFACE

himself of all the love, light, knowledge, and opportunities which may be his for the seeking—who has learned to trust and believe in himself. And miserable and despondent is the mortal who, instead of being self-reliant, talks about his artistic temperament, ignores honest labour, and looks to and depends on other people to do for him that of which he is quite capable himself, but often too tholeless, lazy, and perhaps too superior and heavenly-minded(?) to do for himself.

Correspondents and the Publishers have alike expressed the desire that these lessons should have a wider circulation, and hence this book. The reader will experience the fullest benefits by simply reading one chapter or lesson by itself and putting the suggestions therein into practice for a fortnight, and then pass on to the next chapter and pursue that course of procedure throughout. Its secrets are for those who wish to be benefited by them. All who have adopted the foregoing course have been benefited, in cultivating those qualities in the human mind underlying success in every sphere of life. It deals with the conquest of Self as the essential preliminary to conquest of life. It will help those who mean to help themselves. I trust that these pages, dealing mainly with Self-Reliance, will prove as beneficial to my readers, as the views underlying them have been to correspondents and to myself.

JAMES COATES.

Glenbeg House, Rothesay, Scotland.

Analysis of Contents

CHAPTER II

SELF-RELIANCE OR FAITH IN SELF—*continued*

CHAPTER III

PERSONAL MAGNETISM AND SELF-CULTURE

CHAPTER IV

PERSONAL MAGNETISM AND SELF-CULTURE—*continued*

CHAPTER V

CHAPTER VI

HOW TO CULTIVATE WILL-POWER

CHAPTER VII

HOW TO CULTIVATE WILL-POWER—*continued*

CHAPTER VIII

THE WILL AND ITS DEVELOPMENT

CHAPTER IX

DEFECTS OF WILL, AND HOW TO CURE THEM

CHAPTER X

MODERATION THE KEY TO SELF-CONTROL AND HEALTH

ANALYSIS OF CONTENTS

CHAPTER XIII

CONCENTRATION, ORDER, AND PUNCTUALITY

CHAPTER XIV

SUGGESTION AND ITS APPLICATION

CHAPTER XV

NON-COMATOSE AUTO-SUGGESTION ; PHYSICAL MODES

CHAPTER XVI

NON-COMATOSE AUTO-SUGGESTION (*continued*)—MENTAL MODES

INSOMNIA

AUTO-SUGGESTIONS FOR INSOMNIA

SELF-CONSCIOUSNESS

AUTO-SUGGESTIONS FOR NERVOUS TIMIDITY, SHYNESS, WANT OF CONFIDENCE, BACKWARDNESS, ETC.

SELF-RELIANCE

AUTO-SUGGESTIONS FOR THE CULTIVATION OF SELF-RELIANCE, INCLUDING SELF-ESTEEM, FIRMNESS, COURAGE, AND FAITH IN SELF

Self-Reliance

CHAPTER I

SELF-RELIANCE OR FAITH IN SELF

"Self-reliance and self-denial will teach a man to drink out of
his own cistern, and eat his own sweet-bread, and learn to labour
truly to get his own living and carefully to save and expend the
good things committed to his trust."—LORD BACON.

SELF-RELIANCE is a power of the mind which all possess
in more or less efficiency.   Metaphysicians and cerebral
psychologists have recognised and defined it, and have
given it various names.   To my mind the term "Self-
reliance" is sufficiently comprehensive.   Like every
other power in the mental constitution, Self-reliance
can be cultivated, disciplined, or misused.   Lord Kaimes,
of the old school of metaphysicians, called it "The
Sense of Dignity"; Dr Brown, "Pride"; Reid and
Stewart, "The Desire of Power"; and certainly all these
phases are manifested in Self-reliance.

Whether accepted as "The Desire for Power,"
"Pride," "The Sense of Dignity," or as "Self-esteem,"
it is abundantly clear that among the other good things
committed to man, he is endowed with Self-reliance.

It is implanted in him for his advancement in life. By its rightful exercise he progresses; by its excess he makes an egotistical ass of himself—is arrogant, tyrannical, and unduly estimates his own importance. Lacking in Self-reliance, he fails to make headway in life. There is no strenuous endeavour; none of that excellence of Independence which enjoys best the sweetbread of his own labour; no courageous perseverance, and no success.

Without Self-reliance, progress in any calling in life is impossible. It is a quality more easily pictured in the mind than indicated or defined in exact terms. You may be "well read," intellectual, endowed with fine reasoning powers, and yet lack Self-reliance. You may be something more—a moral man, with distinct longings for attainment in the pure and noble and for the development of all worthy excellencies in yourself, and yet be self-conscious, timid, and wanting in Self-reliance. You may have a strong social nature, and be kindly, considerate and all that, and yet want this desirable mental grit in your disposition, to give "go," purposefulness, and the-never-say-die feature to your disposition. You may be one of the negative "good sort," and mean to do right, but when it comes to doing things, and accepting responsibility, you back down, edge out, and let some one else with stronger convictions, faith, and spirit take your place. It is possible to be a well-doing, well-meaning man, while wanting this quality, or, what is exactly the same, without having cultivated it, although you may have got on well enough till the test came. What form that test has taken, I know not; but lacking Self-reliance, you have broken down. You have not been able to straighten your back, and say "No," when you should have done so. Fear of giving offence, the desire to be considered agreeable, pleasant, and polite, or some such reason has stood in the way; with greater Self-reliance you would have swept these notions to one side, and your "No" would have been "No," and your WILL and POWER TO DO would have been correspondingly reliable.

It is true that no man or woman has ever achieved anything worthy of note, either for others or for themselves, without Self-reliance. But it must· be noted that there have been many, not scholars—probably could not write their name—some, too, with no moral standing to speak of, and whose other characteristics were pretty rough and coarse—these have made headway in their own particular sphere, and have also been able to take care of themselves on their own plane of life. It is clear, however, that the Self-reliance in one's character which is worth having and worthy of development, is that which is associated with all that is best in man. It is not that best, but it is the egotistic sentiment of force by which you put that best into use.

Self-reliance means reliance in one's own powers— independence, self-confidence, dignity, self-sufficiency, and readiness to assume responsibility, which you either possess naturally or which have been educated by the experiences of life, or you have improved by Self-help or Auto-suggestion. Self-reliance is a distinct feature in one's character, derived from observation, reflection, reason or judgment, moral and spiritual tendencies, social nature or sympathies—it is not only the spirit of independence, but it is the possession of dependence on one's self, faith and confidence in the powers within —the divine or spiritual self, which is the real man— and in the subconscious forces, by which the processes of life and all mentation are carried on. It is, therefore, the force of character by which you do things after you have decided upon your line of action.

Self-reliance does not mean mere self-assurance, boasting. The self-reliant man does not boast; he allows his accomplished work and discharge of duty to speak for themselves, should that be necessary. It has nothing to do, as the shallow-minded conjecture, with boasting, aggressiveness, selfish cocksureness, and displays of vanity ; but it means honest dependence on self, which will not ask from others that which can be done by self. It has no time to waste in dreamland and in dependence on others, but *gets up and does.* This Self-reliance is a prize worth possessing. By its legitimate expression you will hold your head high, your conduct will be as erect as your carriage, and even as a commercial asset—by no means to be despised —it has a value convertible into the coin of the realm, which is the gauge by which most men measure success. Self-reliance is not only proper self-respecting pride and dignity, which will not stoop to anything low; it is self-confidence, bravery, courage, determination, and resolution.   It is the power by which, while you think and plan, you screw your courage to the sticking point and take the initiative.   That is surely something of value.   It means that you not only believe in self, as you know yourself, but that you believe in all your God-given powers of spirit, soul, and body—in the dominance of Mind; that you are ready and willing to employ all the qualities of your mind in due order for self-control and self-improvement, and dominate and control your own body.   You will face the difficulties of life and overcome them.   Disappointments will not daunt you.   When encountering difficulties, which possibly have arisen through your own want of fore-sight or other causes, and those which you neither seek nor create, you will pull yourself together and face them bravely, and with set teeth and quiet determina-tion gain the victory.   Opposition merely whets your desire to master it.   You succeed because you have determined to succeed.   That is what I mean by the spirit of Self-reliance, and that is the spirit which is yours to possess if you are so willed.

You may be, as most men are, self-reliant in some things and not in others.   Discover what these latter are, and set about bringing them up to the standard.   In your quiet moments you say to yourself, "I have no difficulty in holding my own privately.   I have opinions which I cherish highly and am ready to defend and maintain, and always do so in my private circle of life, but I have some difficulty in expressing myself clearly and without self-conscious nervousness when in public." Should this be the case, then start about remedying that weak point in Self-reliance. For it is just at this point where you will be most tested in life, and appear less self-reliant than you really are.

Self-reliance, in my opinion, is a mode of motion, *i.e.* functioning of several distinct primary powers of the mind, and not the result of a single faculty. From careful observation I am led to the conclusion that the main factors in Self-reliance are physical health— vigour of brain and body being obvious—and those recognised faculties of the Mind, called Self-esteem, Firmness, Courage, together with a less definable psychical quality, which may be termed Faith in Self.

Physical health—which means good and pure blood —lies at the basis of all vigorous mentation, and certainly is an important factor not only in the manifestation of Self-reliance, but also in all other qualities implanted by the Infinite Spirit in the mental constitution of man, who is recorded to have been created in God's image, having dominion "over every living thing that moveth upon the earth." Man was created, as revealed by his manifest endow- ments, to control or have dominance over himself. Self-denial is merely a method of self-control or education of the Will. The self-reliant man has also the power of self-denial. Following the exercise of

Self-esteem, Firmness, Courage, there is development in that psychic feature called "Faith in Self." There are many phases of faith, as you will know, and of which you will be your own interpreter. There are three phases outstanding: these may be expressed as faith in the Infinite Spirit, the Centre and Source of all that has been, is, or will be; faith in our fellows, by which we credit them with the possession of all ennobling psychical powers, manly worth, probity, etc., or that they are at least inherently capable of all these; also, all that is best in religious, social, and business life is based on that faith. Then comes "Faith in Self." It is an egotistical faith, which believes where it cannot know. It is the faith which says "Here I am, Lord, send me." "I will do it." "I will take the responsibility." "I will see that this is carried out." This faith is not confined to the proconsuls of a great empire, to great travellers and explorers, to notable statesmen and churchmen and ministers, to philanthropists and a host of outstanding advocates of political, moral, and religious liberty, but it is a quality possessed—more or less—by all men and by yourself.

While I deal with the practical side later on in these lessons, I think it necessary to outline Health, Self-esteem, Firmness, Courage, Faith in Self, so that you may enter upon your progress in self-culture in a determined way whenever you propose to put the instructions into practice.

Health of body is the physical foundation of well-being, and is or should be the normal condition of all living creatures. In man, "a sound mind in a sound body" is the state of perfection which should be our aim to possess. Health is largely a constitutional matter, and we inherit it as we do many other physical, mental, and moral conditions, both desirable and undesirable. We inherit, too, long life, as well as tendencies to, and in some cases actual, disease. We also inherit qualities which make for health, success, and well-being. It is yours to modify the unhealthy tendencies, and to make the most of your other good possessions. It would be out of place to deal with the subject of health and the question of treatment here beyond a few hints. I only refer to Health in so far as it relates to Self-reliance and the matters with which I deal in these lessons. I may say in passing that the conditions of health are the opposite of those which cause disease, and no matter what you inherit, it is yours to make the best of your bodily and mental states. The physical conditions of health, next to our constitutional inheritance, are to be found in breathing pure air, drinking pure water, in having an adequate supply of simple and nutritious food; in rest, cleanliness, work or exercise, and in *cheerfulness* —mental attitude—by which to order your ways in a healthy and sensible manner. With some persons, much has been accomplished under great difficulties and in *dis-eased* states of the body; but it stands to reason that good blood makes good health, and with good health and therewith a well-nourished brain, there is strength of body, freedom from pain, and capacity not only to endure hardships, but to enjoy life. With health—the absence of physical *dis-ease*—there is vigour, energy, pith, and force in the body, and the free and harmonious discharge of the various bodily functions, and allied therewith greater force and vim in the brain for the manifestation of mind.

I may observe, in passing, as to the importance of the materials which we require to keep the body in a state of physical health. It is demonstrated by fasting men, patients, and from shipwrecks and mining accidents, that man can live from forty to fifty days without solid food, providing he can get water; but he could not live ten days without water. And we all know that without a good supply of air, the best of water and solid food is of little service. Man can live a long time — comparatively — without food, a shorter time without water, and *no time* without air. "To cease to breathe is to die." To have no air to breathe is practically the same. Impure air is a certain source of disease—one out of the many prevalent causes of disease. To sustain one in physical health, air is of the first importance—good, fresh air in abundance. To obtain full benefit and development, the art of full and correct breathing must be cultivated; men do not breathe enough. The next necessity is water. Man can fast from solid food—and with great advantage at times—but he cannot do without liquids. The quantity as well as the quality is too often overlooked, but it is safe to say "men do not drink enough." Next comes food. With food is the other way about

—for the few who get too little, the majority eat too much ; and with many the *taste* of the food is more important than its good qualities—hence indulgence in much which is both undesirable, unnecessary, and disease-creating. It may therefore be said that too much food, and too little water or drink, are fertile causes of modern physical degeneracy. The breathing of pure air, the freer use of pure liquids—water especially—and the more moderate supply of plain and healthy food must, indeed, be indispensable to any method adopted to maintain and improve health. These, and some useful hints as to work, rest, cleanliness, and mental attitude, will be dealt with in the lessons to follow.

Self-esteem, which is but another name for self-respect, is almost one of the lost virtues, under well-meaning but misguided religious teaching by which self-abasement and self-effacement, called "humility," is lauded as the outward and true sign of all that is good and noble. This humility, so praised, is only another name for cowardice. Children have been whipped, to break their will, for expressing themselves naturally and sensibly, and many a budded genius crushed and the lives of good men and women sacrificed, if not destroyed, by this juggernaut of Sham. Self-depreciation is far too common a habit in all classes. It may be esteemed "good taste," and the acme of all that is virtuous and noble, but it is wholly unnecessary, and an evil suggestion to oneself, which hinders true manly progress and advancement. Manliness, ambition, courage—such highly-lauded virtues—cannot be reconciled with this demoralising self-depreciation, which is at best only the false coin of hypocrites, double-dealers, and tricksters.

Why should it be esteemed a sign of good breeding to extol the talents, ability, goodness and appearance of your fellows, and not only take their coin at face value, but pretend it is worth double, and at the same time depreciate yourself, and assure others that your coin—character, worth, ability—is not worth more than half face value? It may be a sign of good (?) breeding, but it is downright rubbish all the same. To depreciate yourself is about as sensible as to declare your sovereign as only worth ten shillings, and you could not think of allowing your dear friends to accept it for more than that. Of course, no one really believes that about their money. Why, in the name of sound sense, should they expect people to believe it about themselves?

"Great men and women are humble." I believe they are. But no man or woman who has done well for humanity or themselves has lacked Self-reliance, and, consequently, has not been found wanting in Self-esteem. The declaration of Sir Isaac Newton, that he was only like a child picking up shells by the ocean, has been quoted as an evidence of the great man's greater humility. There is no undervaluing, self-abasement, of either himself or of his scientific achievements in the statement. It was rather a manly declaration of the facts. There was an ocean of truth beyond his vision which he had not penetrated, and treasures which he had not salved. And each of us feel and know that we are immersed in and surrounded by eternal mysteries on the psychic side of our nature, and of unsolved systems on the physical; but this does not call for self-depreciation or abasement—personal self-abasement and cant is no part of manliness in any sphere of life, and is as reprehensible as self-laudation.

Do not allow yourself to be misled from the cultivation of a good degree of Self-esteem based on the abuse of the faculty, or upon a misapprehension of its nature. Every man with a moral and intellectual nature will, because of this factor in Self-reliance, command, if not insensibly demand, the respect of his fellows—although relying upon himself—for success in life. It may be that some men with more vanity in their composition than is good for them, and a shallow intellect, are notable for self-conceit, showiness, and those coxcomb and peacock airs which they affect, and which have nothing to do with proper Self-respect or Self-esteem. It may be that some persons whose animal energies are greater than either their intellect or moral character, are domineering and intractable; but this has nothing to do with you—they are labouring under a debased conception of Self-esteem. They reign and tyrannise over those more ignorant than themselves. Do not be affected by these things. Cultivate self-respect, and you will be all the better man for it. Neither pride nor vanity, as these terms are popularly understood, have any place in Self-reliance, in which Self-esteem is such a prominent factor; nor is indifference to the opinions and esteem of one's fellows a feature to be cultivated thereby. Self-reliance has its ambitions, and no ambitious man is indifferent to the support or the good opinion of the world he moves in. His judgment, however, is not overruled by either fear or favour; he *does* that which he knows and believes to be best, unhindered by either.

Should it happen that you have more self-regard than "gumption," more pride than judgment, you may depend on the world to treat you and give you what you are working for, *i.e.* a rude awakening and possibly an empty purse as well. Your vanity without work will not feed you, whatever work will do for you; but if you only work because you must do it to live, you will not do much. On the other hand, you have everything to gain by cultivating a spirit of independence, dignity, self-respect, and masterfulness: to think well of yourself and *live up to it*. Work which has dignity, nobility, and masterfulness—thoroughness—behind it will bring its double reward—increasing power to the worker, and a ready acceptance, commercially, from the world.

Another factor in Self-reliance is Firmness, which gives force, determination, and perseverance, and the "I can and I will" element so much desiderated in these lessons. Bruce is said to have learned his lesson in perseverance from the spider. Perhaps so. It's a very pretty story, anyhow. Life's battles, in whatever sphere, are full of difficulties. Its victories are not for the shirker, dreamer, and loafer—though he be well dressed and pride himself on his handsome appearance—they are for the man who perseveres; they are for the " Try, try again " man, who grows stronger in the trying, as the oak sapling in resisting the blast. To succeed, the source of strength must be in the constitution, as it is in the oak. This faculty of Firmness is in all ; where it is weak it can be cultivated, and where it is in excess it can be subordinated to the judgment. An intractable, positive, stubborn, wilful individual is not a very admirable person, and is not likely to attract either happiness, success, or friends. Firmness is a factor in manliness, and a feature which should be cultivated. These lessons will help you to do so in a quiet, determined way. It is better to have an excess of Firmness than to suffer from a lack of it. Wibbly-wobbly persons, who have no decided mind, are the most difficult to make anything of. They are never successful—" grit," " sand," " steel," are some of the popular expressions indicating Firmness and Courage in a man whom the public admire. In domestic life, no woman can love a man who has no mind of his own—no grit, perseverance, decision. And in every sphere of life Firmness, subordinated to judgment—disciplined by experience and possibly by self-help processes—is a virtue. Stubbornness is simply the manifestation of Firmness under the selfish dominance of passion, offended vanity, or other lower quality of man. Such folly eventually brings its own reward. To be firm,

decided, deliberate, persevering, are essentially qualities of all that is manly.

Thousands of able, clever young fellows have drifted
on the sea of life, or for a time made a great show of
sail—something attractive in style—and have either
failed or made complete shipwreck, for want of Firmness, or want of its exercise when most required.
Failures through want of perseverance are too common;
perseverance, application, staying power are just so
many features of Firmness.

The kind of Self-reliance which enabled Luther to go
to Worms, if there were as many devils there as tiles on
the housetops; or Wilberforce to face countless enemies
and prejudices in the advocacy of anti-slavery, and
which it is desirable a man should have,—possesses in
addition to Self-respect and Firmness another quality,
that of Courage. Courage is an element in the human
constitution distinct from the intellectual and moral
powers. A brute may be courageous, but that does not
detract from its value as a great and important element
of human character. Self-reliance without Courage
would be like salt without savour. Courage shows itself
in resistance, in defence, in pluck, in staying powers;
sometimes in defiance, and always in self-protection
(which includes not only the individual—his household,
wife and children—goods and chattels); also in a larger
sense in his ideals—faith in God, love of country or
cause, and in the defence of friends, etc. The practical
side of Courage is as much intended to conserve business
interests and other private states in life—social and

domestic affairs—as for use in the more public offices
and arena of life. It is essential to force of character.
Without intellectual direction, unsustained by moral
and spiritual considerations and lacking the modifying
influence of domestic affections, Courage may, allied
to more undesirable features, partake of the nature
of quarrelsomeness, contentiousness, and fault-finding.
But these abuses and misconceptions should not prevent you from aiming at the cultivation of a bright,
courageous spirit: the power to defend a principle or a
possession—TO DO, AND NOT TO REFRAIN FROM DOING
WHAT IS RIGHT. There is no need to go out of your way
to prove that you are courageous. Reserve it for use
when it is wanted, but see that you have it. Don't
run away under the plea of humility, modesty,
expediency, sensitiveness, when you should be true to
your conscience or colours. Better be courageous—
under a misconception of what is right—than be
a trifler, a shirker of responsibilities, a creature
wanting in spirit and force of character, in the hour
of need.

To be courageous, begin with yourself: force yourself
to go forward when you would hold back, to do when
you would refrain, to speak when you would be silent,
or silent when you would speak—with want of judgment or knowledge of facts—and in a little you will be
energetic in carrying out your plans, or orders entrusted
to you. Cultivate a courageous, resolute, manly spirit.
It is nothing to you that there is a lot of pseudo-
courage in the world, bombast, tyranny, and of the

downright-selfish-might-is-right-character.   Do not let this hinder you making the best of what is in yourself and in your circumstances.   You will need Courage for that, and see that you develop it.   One-half of the battle lies in the conviction that you have right on your side, and the other half in the sincere conviction that the right is worth fighting for.   You cannot be thorough without Courage ; without thoroughness there can be no success.   If you are physically blind, no blame to you if you cannot see ; if you are lame, you will not be chided for not being able to race ; if you are idiotic, no one will object to your weak will ; but you will be handicapped all the same.   There are many men who are never blind, lame, nor idiotic, yet deliberately handicap themselves in life for want of Courage.   Don't be one of these.   "Whatsoever your hands find to do, that do with all your might," is the language of Courage. Given two men of equal intellectual ability, the one with a good share and the other with much less of the element called Courage, you may safely forecast who will turn out best.   Efficiency, even in a quiet sphere of life, is impossible without Courage.   I therefore think that Courage is an essential factor in Self-reliance.   In the development of Self-reliance as set forth in these lessons, you will improve your physical health, mental vigour, and your own self-respect, confidence, Firmness, and Courage.

There is a quality in the mental constitution which we recognise as the power of Concentration.   It is allied to Firmness.   While the latter gives steadiness and perseverance, the former indicates the power of application in a given direction. This will be treated elsewhere. Meantime, the following suggestion is worthy of attention:—

"In whatever you engage, pursue it with a steadiness of purpose as though you were determined to succeed. A vacillating mind never accomplished anything worth naming. There is nothing like a fixed, steady aim; it dignifies our nature and ensures our success. Who has done most for mankind? Who have secured the rarest honours? Who have raised themselves from poverty to riches? Those who were steady to their purposes. The man who is one thing to-day and another to-morrow—who drives an idea pell-mell this week, while it drives him next week—is always in trouble, and does nothing from one year's end to the other. Look at and admire the man of steady purpose. He moves noise-lessly along; and yet what wonders he accomplishes! He rises gradually, we grant, but surely."

Now picture to your mind's eye the self-reliant man of backbone and purpose, and a man of opposite disposition. Make your selection, and you will naturally choose to be the former—the self-reliant man. Picture yourself as a self-reliant man—one who does things for the best and because it is the best, without waiting with bowed head to get permission, or the favour of your fellows to get a hearing or get support—and you will be putting yourself in the footsteps of all great and good men who have dared to think for themselves, and to lead—who were successful because they made themselves capable of succeeding. Think of yourself as self-reliant. Put this Self-reliance into practice from time to time, and you will know something of that *inner force*, which I call Faith in Self, and which will give you undoubted Courage in the face of difficulties, and mastership of self.

CHAPTER II

" In the toil and sweat of my younger days I knew that a time
  would come
  When I'd press the throat of a thing called Fate with a master's
  despot thumb.
  And to-day I say, in a ringing line of proud, exultant truth,
  That success is sure for the heart that throbs with the spirit of
  living youth ! "   GRANT HARVEY.

SELF-RELIANCE is essential to progress in every sphere
of life, in the playing fields as well as in the study.   It
is essential to thoroughness, self-possession, presence of
mind, and enthusiasm—because it partakes of vital
vigour and nervous energy, usually and succinctly
expressed as " go."

The noted statesman, churchman, legal dignitary,
scientist, psychologist, commander of armies, admiral of
the fleet, bishop, parson, as well as soldier, sailor,
cashier, or salesman, may be, as many are, keen golfers,
cricketers, lawn-tennis or football players, wherein
Self-reliance is as much exhibited as in the more serious
pursuits in life.   Life would be made more thoroughly
enjoyable had folk sense enough to impart more Self-
reliance into work as well as play; for the former has
its joys as well as the latter.

Mr C. B. Fry, the well-known athlete and journalist, in a recent number of his Magazine referred to the Hon. Francis Stanley Jackson as "a great cricketer." He stands in the front rank as a batsman and bowler, and this means the possession of imperturbable decision, alertness, quickness in forming judgment, with promptness of action and all that.   But he is not only a great cricketer, captain of the England Eleven, but he is also the brains of an important business in Leeds, and a director of the *Yorkshire Post*, Limited.   In work as in play, what is the secret of his success ?   Self-reliance —a quality which he has in a large degree.   And what is the secret of his Self-reliance by which he keeps himself up to the mark ?   C. B. Fry answers (page 490, No. 18, vol. iii.): "Stanley Jackson is a living example, as a batsman, of the power of unconscious Autosuggestion.   He tells himself unconsciously that determined concentration has nothing to fear from any bowling; *and he does what he tells himself to do.*   It is called 'confidence.'"

The man who would succeed in life must cultivate this Faith or Confidence in himself.

Now please note : cultivation means practice or work, *i.e.* the Auto-suggestion of determined concentration put into practice.   Whether you are writing a letter, answering a question, directing an undertaking, receiving or executing orders; or, possibly, in the playing fields of life, recreating, resting, sleeping—tell yourself " to be thorough," and put your best into what you are at, and this faith, "confidence" (which is another name for

Self-reliance), will become stronger and more perfect day by day.

Faith in Self is of necessity an essential feature in Self-reliance, and this faith is a matter of growth, confidence begetting confidence, success commanding success. It may not be as clearly expressed as realised. Thus the boy who timorously stands on the banks of a stream, or is venturing his first dip in the sea, may not be able to express clearly what his introspections relating thereto were; he has been fearful, doubting himself, but he sees other lads run or plunge in and come out none the worse, but supremely cheerful and buoyant. He summons courage with an effort, and discovers that his fears were practically groundless. He is able to accomplish and enjoy, and even in time he is able to excel others. Faith in Self is a matter of growth, but that growth must have a beginning. There is a period—and periods—when there must be decision to start. That first step taken, difficulties—seeming and real—depart, and successful achievement eventually results. That is one way of looking at Faith in Self.

Faith in Self, as a factor in Self-reliance, has a broader basis than many realise. It is a growth based on an infinite variety of experiences which have borne steady testimony to its value. And owing to its possession, you are spurred on by the thought, "I have been successful in the past—I overcame all the difficulties—and now I am determined to go on with new ventures." And so you proceed to the accomplishment of some other tasks in which you have had no experience; and with increased Self-reliance, you now diligently undertake them. If you are in employment and are told to do a certain thing, you do not hang back, persuading yourself you are incapable. If you are a man or esteemed a man, you will trust yourself, promptly obey, and do your level best. Faith in Self grows in proportion not only to past experiences, where properly directed effort has been rewarded by success, but also in proportion to an increased knowledge of oneself. It is true that reflection in the quiet hours recalls the lessons of experience; it does more for those who really take time to reflect—it brings to mind the deeper, broadening conceptions of oneself, of one's powers. This is especially true with the man who, while endeavouring to overcome a defect or vice in himself, gains a deeper insight into his own powers; and realises the ability to do things which he had either not thought of attempting, or probably imagined impossible. His increased faith came from increased knowledge of himself. And because of this faith he accepts responsibility to accomplish that for which his knowledge has yet to be gained.

There is a moral, mental, and spiritual conception of self, of which in the earlier stages only fitful glimpses were obtained; but as we progress, we learn more and rejoice, as the timid boy did when he first realised he could really *do* that which he was at first afraid to attempt. The pushful, hustling, all-sails-set individual, taking little time for reflection, and none for real self-control and development, knows nothing of this side of his nature.

In this cursory and brief view of Faith in Self as a factor in Self-reliance, it is to be remembered that this faith is a matter of growth, and is based on a conscious beginning—an effort—fed by our experience, even as confidence begets confidence and success, success, in the estimate of practical realisation. But it is more than this, it is a growth based on a wider and more comprehensive knowledge of ourselves, from reflection on and introspection of the possibilities of our moral and spiritual nature, and our relation to the Source of all Power. The child walks at first by clinging to the finger of the mother, and unconsciously by growth and practice comes the period of effort—the determination to walk unaided physically, but encouraged and mentally supported as yet by the presence of that mother, and, finally, by Self-reliance. There may have been difficulties and drawbacks, and many mishaps, in the process; yet these, instead of being real hindrances, were aids in the growth of greater determination and further effort, till success was achieved and the victory assured.

As the child with the parent, so are we in relation to the Infinite Source of all life and good, of which we are a part and by which we are sustained and protected. We have our periods of difficulties and drawbacks, wherein we stumble and fail; but these do not really hinder our progress so long as we have faith in that greater-self, by which we are ever in touch with the Infinite Source of all life, all good, and all strength. Every effort, every determination, every demand on that Source is ours now to possess, as surely as the mother's love, strength, and protection is there to infuse and sustain the growing strength and developing powers of the child.

By Faith in Self I mean something more than mere self-sufficiency, based on a sort of ignorant cocksureness; faith in the superior powers—implanted by the Infinite, and possessed by each—we can by steady, persistent, and conscious effort deliberately bring into play, and with greater assurance of success, because of our Self-reliance therein. It is no more derogatory to the Supreme to have faith in ourselves, than it is to the parent when the boy, because of it, takes his first plunge into the water, or into business and other pursuits, the performance of which reflects credit upon the powers which he possesses, and the exercise of which materially increases his ability for further achievements.

By Faith in Self you get at your best within the limits and possibilities of your constitution. You get the best out of life for which you are fitted, and you grow in grace to a higher, wider, and more comprehensive knowledge of yourself, position and rights, in the order of your being. In fact, you learn to know yourself more comprehensively — your duties, your powers, and the force and courage of your being. Where you may in the past have been indifferent, idle, or retrogressive, you will *now advance*, not because you know what the result will be; you will not hold back because your ideas meet with rebuffs ; you have Faith in Self to accomplish that which you have decided to undertake — a strong faith which enables you to plunge into the unknown, as Stanley the explorer into tropical, untrodden forests in pursuit of the mission which he had faith not only in himself to carry out but faith in the ultimate accomplishment of his purpose. He had faith not only in the practical man of daily experience, but in the intuitive man—the greater or real self behind, which is in touch with the soul-consciousness of things. Stanley was the last man on earth given to mysticism or occultism, but he had faith. He not only learned to control himself and others, but he had learned to know and appreciate a greater self than the ordinary conscious man of action— that is, the man of intuition, faith, and Spirit, who brings us into touch with powers unseen which at times overshadow and direct us, where experience and knowledge fail us.

Faith in Self is no figment, but a powerful reality, and by its aid we demand success. The "gaun fit aye gets " is a Scotch proverb, signifying the reward of endeavour based on Faith in Self. You have a right to demand success. It is your duty as well as your privilege to claim it, but sometimes we not only neglect to do so, but what is worse, we neglect *to demand success in ourselves.* We have it in us to succeed, and do not succeed because we fail to properly appreciate ourselves, and bring into action that which is best in us.

Now let us see what this Faith in Self means :—It means an optimistic faith in not only the whole man—known and unknown—the man you know of conscious daily experience, but the unknown man with all potentialities and powers yet to be developed and called into play—your Faith in Self, and in the source of all your powers by which you are "I am," a living, sentient, individualised part. This is no idle, bombastic faith. It is a sober faith, founded on a sincere conviction of man's high estate as the offspring of the Infinite, as a son of God ; a man, with all his God-given powers of spirit, soul, consciousness, brain, intellect, body, and estate. It is a faith which honours the Creator and ennobles the man. It gives pause in excitement, coolness in difficulties, presence of mind in sudden disasters, and enables you to gird up your loins and come to the attack again and again till victory or death in arms is assured. It is the faith that does and dares, the faith which raises " the banner of I will and I can." It attempts and perseveres, because it believes in the full and the right use of all the powers of our being. While the majority are making haste to get rich, or going mad after amusements, it is going quietly to work to get the best out of oneself. It certainly does not shirk work, neither does it become a slave to work ; much less a slave to passions and appetites. It will have nothing to do with riches or enjoyment at the cost of either health, the waste of power, or the loss of one's self-respect, for all that is manly and worthy.

Many a man even when industrious and studious, and gifted with many excellencies, hangs behind and waits to be recognised and taken up, and is handicapped simply and solely from want of Faith in Self, while the less gifted, but not less industrious, march forward and succeed. If you think this is too big a claim, I will modify it and say—*they march forward and are more successful than those who refrain from the attempt* through want of this absolutely necessary and thoroughly honest faith. Believe in yourself—

"Nothing ventured, nothing won."

Although this may be regarded nowadays as a gambling and speculative phrase, it is applicable here. If there is a thing which you realise you can do better than another, THAT DO; AND DO NOT REFRAIN FROM DOING EITHER FROM SOME EGOTISTICAL SELF-CONSCIOUSNESS OF MENTAL SUPERIORITY, REFINEMENT, SENSITIVENESS TO YOUR FELLOW-CREATURES, OR SOME FALSE MODESTY WHICH PREVENTS THE PERFORMANCE. Do not act the part of the spoiled child—so shy—"I don't like to." This is not the way "forlorn hopes" are led, victories gained, businesses made, professional honours achieved, social improvements undertaken, personal character redeemed, and success obtained.

"I CAN," "I WILL," "I MUST," "I AM ABLE," are the unspoken expressions of one who seizes the nettle boldly, and is not stung. "I am afraid," "I am not sure," "I'd rather not," "I think you had better do it" —this is neither the language of faith nor of willingness to succeed; it plays with the nettles of difficulty in life, and gets stung every time. This want of Faith in Self is not only dishonouring to manly worth and the possibilities of man, but also to the Source of Being, from which man derives all his invaluable powers, which he often altogether fails to appreciate, and does little or nothing to develop.

When you realise truly your relation to the Over-Soul—to your own spiritual self and psychic powers—and the fact that there can be no existence apart from the Infinite Source of all good, power, and perfection, and that all are governed by immutable laws which ever work for your good—growth, progress, and develop-ment—it is yours to advance and make the best of life. Rest assured that you will advance by bending yourself to the task, or you will assuredly take a retrogressive course, with all the stultification and misery which that brings, not only to yourself, but all who are in touch with you. You will surely choose that which is best for the conscious and deliberate improvement of yourself—buoyed up with the faith of sure and certain progress, through the development of the inherent potentialities of your being, of which you are already slowly but certainly becoming to know more.

Faith in Self is a stimulation to the putting forth, persistently and deliberately, of all your known powers, sustained by the conviction that if you do so you will develop these, and bring more fully into play your subconscious forces and latent potentialities, and also demand from the Unseen and the hidden sources of being—and all which that means—greater power still to make progress in life. We are created for a wise purpose, and have a right to demand the good; and one form that demand takes, is to honour the good within and live up to it.

Leaving what seems to be occult and mystic on the one hand, we learn by the exercise of our known powers to improve them, and are stimulated thereto by faith in the Unseen Source whose indestructible, immortal forces are the very essence of our being. This faith in the Unseen and also in ourselves, in whom these forces constitute our real inward and essential self, cannot be otherwise than an elevating faith— influencing and ennobling our life and character. This is a steady conviction which will lead to the perfection of the individual—it will lead to your advancement now, and whatever you decide on in the secret silence of your nature—the closet wherein you pray and meditate will be realised in your daily life.

Believe in yourself—the greater the belief, the greater will be the accomplishment.

If you realise your will is weak, you can set to work to improve it. Should you discover that your powers of concentration are spasmodic, you will be able, by making the effort to call in your wandering thoughts to the peaceful centre of desire, to train and develop them and send them forth in an orderly and deliberate fashion. The mariner does not create the winds of heaven or the currents of the sea, but by faith and knowledge he steers his bark. So may you steer your bark to the haven of health, happiness, and success by the discipline of your will, the culture of your intellect, the exercise of your sympathetic moral and spiritual forces, which this Faith in Self believes, and past experience has proved possible.

Have faith in yourself, and that faith by the laws of sympathy, association, intuition—telepathy, if you will—will communicate itself to others, and bring you and them into confidence and support. Those in sympathy with you will join their mental forces to yours and unconsciously assist your progress. As you evolve the best in you, negative and unsuccessful thoughts within you will be replaced with positive, earnest, determined thoughts which make for success. "The less you depend upon others and the more you trust your enlightened reason, the clearer you will see and the more strength you will have to stand alone. You will realise that as an inseparable part of the Infinite power of good, you may command the qualities needed to accomplish wonderful results. You will receive an impulse and an inspiration that will be finer and more effective. You will advance to higher planes of usefulness and grow in knowledge and understanding."

So much for Faith in Self. What I have not made clear you can think out for yourself. That is the way of success. Think for yourself, and keep on believing in yourself, and work, live up to your thinking. Faith in Self is not health, wealth, success, usefulness, or happiness—so much *coveted* by many, without the labour or the living for—but Faith in Self

is one of the factors in mental endeavour which enable
you to demand and have that which is best in these.
You may be helped in life by such aids as education—
science, religion, art—by good, useful, healthy companion-
ships, all of which you will be wise, so far as lies in
your power, to make use of ; but without a good, honest,
optimistic Faith in Self, you will do little towards
achieving success, and making the best out of life.

Presuming self-confidence is the badge of the fool;
but self-confidence, which gives dignity to character
and shows itself in a straight, honest, cheerful and
industrious life, is the badge of the man.

Picture to your mind's eye yourself as a healthy man,
who lives, moves, and has his being in a physically and
mentally healthy atmosphere. Recall to yourself the
healthiest and brightest moments of your life—the
cleanest, most helpful moments—and think over them,
with all the joyous sensations which memory spurred to
action can recall. Then determine in your mind to be
a healthy and a clean man physically, to abstain from
thoughts and things which degrade, and so order your
life in thought that you may have the greatest good
out of it. Perhaps you are not just as healthy as you
might be. In that case make up your mind to be
healthy ; a clean, temperate life will work wonders,
and see that you use the means. Lay a good foundation
in physical health. The attempt will not interfere
with either work or enterprise, but will enhance your
powers for their accomplishment.

Then see yourself, not only a healthy man, but a self-reliant one, with something of honest faith in yourself. Let your chest be expanded with the sweet air of heaven—freely and fully expand your lungs, and assume the manly attitude of one who feels and knows that he has a right to live, that there is good material in him, and you are determined to make the best of that. Carry your head erect, and let it sit straight on your neck, *with mouth shut*, chin in, and the crown of your head towards heaven, and not pointed at some impossible horizon or arc of the heavens in front of you. Put your foot firmly on the earth, and for ever have done with shuffling and feeble knees. Let there be a firm grip in your hand, brightness in your eye, cheerfulness in your voice, and a determination to do and to dare in your soul, as one who has awakened to the fact that you have discovered several good-paying lodes in yourself and you are going to work them for all they are worth—get the gold, although you have to work hard to get rid of the dirt. Faith in yourself will be the weapon by which you will forge your way and overcome all difficulties. So far so good; and while you are thinking of that which you are determined to achieve, *do not neglect the present.* If you have Faith in Self, show it in the discharge of present duties, in faithful and willing service. It is the work of to-day and the spirit in which that work is done which fits for better things to-morrow. There is no false pride in Self-confidence. It is never ashamed in being caught at work; it does not make excuses and apologies at being caught with the jacket off, or the sleeves rolled up—not a bit of it. It means to make those a stepping-stone to better things. See yourself cheerfully at work with an eye to the future, but with no neglect of the present. The spirit of health, vigour, diligence, will carry you through.

As self-reliant, you have no truckling with a weak, fawning spirit—such Help is not in your line. You see yourself respectful, courteous, prompt, and willing, and, above all, as a man of faith in yourself you are calm, clear-headed, and self-controlled. You are more: you have something of that Personal Magnetism which attracts success. Your Self-reliance unconsciously begets confidence in others, and your Personal Magnetism attracts. These are the switches by which you place yourself in touch with the spiritual and subconscious forces within and above you, in yourself and others. By your manliness, dignity, and straightforwardness, you draw to yourself kindred souls with similar honest and praiseworthy characteristics. You consciously lay yourself out for the best, and you will get it. You have possibly made many beginnings, but resolve now *within yourself* to make a fresh start and wisely keep it up, as a man with a healthy motive. Help yourself. These pages will help you. Begin now.

THINK OVER IT, AND WHAT YOU CONSCIOUSLY DETERMINE TO CONSISTENTLY AND PERSISTENTLY KEEP IN VIEW, YOU WILL BECOME. .

IT IS THE "I WILL" MAN WHO DOES.

THE MAN WHO SAYS THAT HE HAS FAITH IN HIMSELF,

BUT WHO WILL NOT WORK, DECEIVES HIMSELF. YOU PROVE YOUR FAITH BY YOUR WORKS.

THINK HEALTH; LIVE HEALTH AND YOU WILL BE HEALTHY.

THINK AND PONDER ON SELF-RELIANCE, PRACTISE IT, AND YOU WILL BE SELF-RELIANT.

THINK SUCCESS, WORK FOR SUCCESS, AND YOU WILL BE SUCCESSFUL.

HEALTH, WEALTH, HAPPINESS, WISDOM, NOBILITY, GLORY, AND MANHOOD ARE YOURS JUST AS SURELY AS YOU BELIEVE IN THEM AND DEMAND THEM BY YOUR APPLIED ENERGIES.

THINK IN A YOUTHFUL, BRIGHT, JOYFUL SPIRIT, AND YOU WILL BE YOUTHFUL, BRIGHT AND JOYFUL IN SPIRIT AND SHED HAPPINESS ALL AROUND YOU, WHILE EXULTING IN THE JOY OF LIFE.

Think these things out, ponder over them, determine as others have done successfully TO BE THEM, and by and by you will rejoice in being able to realise how much you have achieved by honest and persistent endeavour, founded on manly Self-reliance.

CHAPTER III

"The way to wealth is as plain as the way to market; it depends chiefly on two words—industry and frugality—that is, waste neither time nor money, but make the best use of both. Without industry and frugality nothing will do, and with them everything."—FRANKLIN.

WHAT is Personal Magnetism? That is a question which cannot be directly answered. It is a subtle influence which you appreciate, feel, and imagine, but what it really is you do not exactly know and cannot well define. These lessons are not only a practical answer to the question, but a guide to the possession of the coveted power and an aid to success in life. All strong, emotional, and self-controlled natures possess it for good or ill. Men and women of strong faith, convictions, reveal it. It conquers, wins, attracts, and dominates those less endowed with it. We are convinced of strength, purpose, determination, and above all Self-reliance, in those who possess it. Whether a Grant or a Kitchener, Joan of Arc or a Florence Nightingale, a Roberts or a Cronje, a Parker or a Brooke, an Oliver Lodge or a "Mark Twain," however differing in intellect, outlook, or motives, we find them possessed of the indefinable influence—Personal Magnetism—which stamps them with power.

Personal Magnetism is an Americanism for personality which is attractive, masterful, magnetic, which we all recognise in thought but find it so difficult to define. A person may be neither handsome, well-built, nor yet scholarly, and yet be most winsome, attractive, and masterly. But it is certain that *nous*—judgment and intuition—tact, decision of character, straightforwardness, moral stamina, perseverance, self-reliance, self-control, *reserve*, sound temper, patience, a saving sense of humour, and a fairly sound constitution, are some of the qualities which make the individual magnetic and attractive. A well-formed brain and a healthy physique are, in my opinion, the foundations of a strong personality. Much can be done to improve both, and in this, as in other things, WHERE THERE IS A WILL, THERE IS A WAY.

Personal Magnetism is the power of powers. Without it there is no genius, little talent, and less success. With it all things are possible. The Senate listens and is led. Men obey; women are silent and attentive— and govern by the exercise of similar powers—and the possessor becomes a centre of power. He attracts and governs; is conscious of his own powers; is clear-sighted and self-reliant, and is prepared to cope with emergencies as they arise. Riches cannot purchase it, but *all* may have it who *want* it and *work* for it. It is the fruitage of a vigorous mind and a healthy body.

Some are more richly endowed than others, but you

can rest assured it is not for the dreamer, the drone, and the shuffler. The thinker and the worker *with an aim in life*, is already possessed of it, and will succeed in proportion as he is able to employ it. If you want to succeed in life, the following hints may help you. And what is more, they will help you in proportion as you take yourself, firmly with both hands, and thus help yourself to put the advice given into practice. I may say in passing that there is no relation between Personal Magnetism and terrestrial magnetism, although the latter may be used to illustrate the power which in man is a vibrant vital energy, generated in the physical organisation from pure air, pure water, suitable diet moderation, and whatever in the way of sensible living and exercise with self-control best contributes to the well-being and health of the individual.

A great deal which has been written on this subject of late years might be called "Transcendental hash" or "Transatlantic gush," with its pretensions to Occultism and other wonderful short-cuts to the attainment of knowledge, power, unlimited health, wealth, success, beauty, and all that. What you want is something practical.

To succeed in life, you must work; to attain, you must put yourself in the way of attainment. This is best done by having, in the first place :—

(*a*) A reasonable knowledge of your own qualifications, your *bent*, and what you have done in the past to either hinder or advance yourself.

(*b*) In quietly determining to improve your powers.

(c) In realising the world's need of your abilities, which includes *your need* of them.

(d) In having the open eye for opportunities, and making the best use of these; and finally, where there is a lack of opportunity, *make it*.

There is nothing very mystic, occult, or even new in these suggestions, but in practice, which is the main thing, they will be found to work out all right.

To place yourself in the way of attainment, almost spells success. Of examples there are many. Better to chop wood, and do it well, than be an indifferent actor just with go enough to "speak a piece" and walk through it. To give oneself airs, wear a fancy coat, and give oneself a high-sounding name do not help one, and yet the "Profession" is full of these vain triflers—full of words, words, words, but poor in performance—who will ultimately swell the ranks of the unemployed. Actors who succeed—in one of the most difficult of arts — are those who are diligent, shirk not hard work, in learning the smallest part— "doing the smalls"—at small salaries, and hence are ready when the opportunity comes of seizing it.

Opportunity is a great factor in success. But opportunity only comes to those on the *qui vive*—on the lookout.

"One of the greatest actors in America," says Mr Charles Hawtrey in *The Grand Magazine*, "might still be playing small parts in Stock companies had not one of his fellow-actors thrown up his part in the production of a new play in New York some time ago.

The actor, who is now in the very front rank of American managers, offered himself for the part, and in one night made a name for himself, which is second to none in the United States. Here is an instance of what opportunity does, if a young actor ' takes it at the flood.' "

Charles Kean and the late Sir Henry Irving are outstanding examples.

What is true of the stage is true of commerce. The young man who is intent on holidays, who has a feeling that he is altogether too good for either his work, his salary, or for " that old skinflint " his master, and therefore takes but little interest in the business and is only concerned to get through " his bit," and no more, courts failure—and gets it. Where there is no living interest, there is no Personal Magnetism.

A special article appeared in a recent issue of the *London Evening News*. It was entitled " A Word to the Junior Clerk, by the Senior Partner," and admirably illustrates the way of attainment. It showed how the office boy more frequently becomes the head of the firm than the junior clerk. The former begins at the beginning, and is not above his work. His training is more thorough. He climbs to the top of the ladder, while the junior clerk sticks somewhere on the way. Shorthand, typewriting, and a knowledge of a foreign language are recommended as a means to an end. These are valuable tools in the hands of ability, but not much use to the idle and shiftless who only want to get through anyhow. The writer of the article tells

how he learned French when young, and he was close
on thirty before he reaped much benefit. A Paris
customer was in the chief's room with the chief and
himself. He had been talking French with the
customer on the way up. The caller suddenly said to
his chief: "Ellison, why don't you send this young
gentleman over to Paris and pension off poor old
Whiteman? He speaks French perfectly." He got
the post of representative in Paris for the house.
French, without business ability—fitness—would not
have helped him. He had both, and when the opportunity came he was able to take it with both hands,
and succeed.

The present head of a most successful firm of
publishers in London, entered the place as an office
boy in 1880. Parents well disposed, but poor in circumstances, were glad of the help which his small
wage gave. This youth improved himself: learned
shorthand, and in due time was able to attend to some
correspondence. Then was called upon to report
lectures and do other work for the firm. Although
there were many changes in the firm's employees, he
—without influence—remained and advanced. When
openings came he stepped into them, and gradually had
full charge of the commercial department. Became a
partner with a quarter interest: his capital, part
savings and part service. In a few years obtained a
half interest. Later still the two remaining partners,
for business and family reasons, wished to take up
special work with their publishing branch in New York,

and this gentleman, the former office boy, was able to arrange and take over the whole business, now one of the most successful in London. He had ability, and worked it up. His capital was character and Personal Magnetism. He was trusted, and attracted confidence.

The qualities which make for success in the army are:—Fitness for work. The doing of it with alacrity. Promptitude and qualifying for the service by learning each detail, and putting the *esprit de corp*, with duty, before any other consideration. The time has gone by for a purse to purchase the next step, or make a fool a General on the strength of £5000 a year. Major-General Sir Alfred Turner, K.C.B., late Inspector-General of the Auxiliary Forces at the War Office—a soldier who was promoted from time to time, without the slightest influence at or on the Military Head-quarters, and without means, save £60 per annum, from his father in the early stages of his career—is one of the many instances of what *grit*, determination, and faithfulness to duty can do for a man, even in military service—the most difficult, and full of the most execrable and unexpected surprises.

Sir Ian Hamilton, one of the strong, *silent* men of the British Army—whose splendid record is the outcome of initiative and not of back-stairs influence—in his *Staff-Officer's Scrap Book* says :—

" The best qualification for success seems, then, to be not to desire it over-anxiously ; and certainly the best moments in life are not those in which a man sees

PERSONAL MAGNETISM & SELF-CULTURE 43

success impending, still less those in which he savours
the Dead Sea Fruit of achievement with its sickly
complementary sauce of congratulations and applause.
*Are they not those moments in which it is borne into a
poor mortal that some immortal has designated the field
of action, wherein he has only to be true to his convictions
and himself, and advance confidently by the word of
command to the accomplishment of some predestined end?"*
(The italics are mine.)

The foregoing suggests the SPIRIT with which to
accept the command to go forward in life—without
over-anxiety.   Do your part ; learn to do it, and when
the time comes act with promptitude, without question,
as a man true to his own convictions.

Take the all-embracing sphere of mechanics.   The
youth who enters one or other branches of the industry,
and whose aim is to get through his apprenticeship
somehow, becomes an animated tool—a slight addition
to the mechanical and engineering appliances by which
he is surrounded.   He may possibly be called a good
workman, but he will be nothing more.   Probably he
will drop out of the running, as one who finds "a job
hard to get."   He has gone about his work in the
wrong spirit.   There is no go, enthusiasm, interest,
and consequently no intelligent appreciation.   Apart
from fitness, his emotions lean in other directions;
hence his failure, or comparative failure.   He has
failed to master his profession ; or if he has, he is not
a success, through the dominance of some emotion,
passion, or appetite which he gratifies, but does not

control, and is therefore not only unable to make progress in his profession, but in life.

Are you a musician? You could not be that unless you had "the ear." But no amount of ear would be of any service without interest, shown in diligent and almost daily practice. Education, masterly technique, count for something, but without the Spirit the music is without soul. It does not touch the emotions and kindle its own response in those who hear it. That life, that Spirit, comes from that X-force of the emotions, which distinguishes one man—aye; and woman—from another—Personal Magnetism.

Here we have several factors: "the ear," the practice of musical training, and the Personal Magnetism. Given these three things, when the opportunity comes it will be seized, and "worked for all its worth." That way success lies.

If you want to be the master of men, be first the master of Self. The civilian has his battleground as well as the soldier. Each requires special qualities for his work, but the victory is for the "Do-and-dare" and "Never-say-die" man. Strength of character is essential to success, and that strength of character is equal to its weakest link. Look this fact straight in the face—your strength is equal to that. Apparently great men have failed, just amid the plaudits of their fellows and the world's admiration or fear—*they failed because of some secret habit, constituting the weakest link in their character.* What is that link? Don't shirk the task. Look for it and cut it out, and your chain of manhood and being will be all the better without it.

Strength of body is something ; physical courage is a valuable asset; but the whole is useless without *the moral courage* which inspires, by which one acts with decision when the opportunity comes. Great enterprises require great men and great responsibility, relentless vigour, and greater resolution. But you are not a great man. Your aim is to be a man. You have some experience of life. You know that it is better to play one tune well than half a dozen indifferently. Great enterprises may not be yours to carry through, but you are wise enough to know that lesser enterprises, *safely carried through at all costs*, are a thousand times better than a magnificent conception which you have failed to realise through vacillation, want of purpose, pluck, spirit—Moral Courage, Faith in Self, or Self-reliance, which men feel and recognise as Personal Magnetism.

A special taste, willingness to learn, zeal and obedience, industry, method, perseverance, moral courage, bodily health and strength, are some of the qualities which make for success, and these should be cultivated assiduously.

There is no such word as FAIL in the Golden Lexicon of the student of Personal Magnetism— whether he learns the lesson at twenty or sixty. He fears no man. He fears not for himself. He relies on himself, making the best use of that which is within his reach. Whether with a bugle, or with bayonet or

sword in hand; behind a desk or counter, or at a
bench; down a mine, or with his finger on the throttle-
valve of a locomotive—whatsoever post or position it be
his to fulfil, he is alert, "all there," ambitious and
purposeful. He is not waiting for people to give him
a lift, or depending on his parents to keep him when
he should be his own supporter and the mainstay for
others. *He is magnetic; he is a success.*

It was an ambition of the Right Hon. John Burns,
when a poor lad, to be Member of Parliament; it was not
an idle ambition, for he worked diligently and fearlessly,
and made the most of his opportunities by being both
diligent in his work and in the improvement of his
mental powers. The foundation which he laid by
making full use of his chances—scanty enough at times
—made his castle in the air become a realisation. One
day while helping his mother to bring home some wash-
ing from a house in Park Lane and they were passing
the Houses of Parliament, John Burns turned to his
mother and said: "When I am in there, mother, you
shall not have to work as hard as you do now." As we
all know, these truly prophetic words have been fulfilled. The boy had the ambition, and he succeeded
because he left nothing to chance—luck, as some call
it—but pegged away with moral energy, and a true
manly spirit at what was nearest to him. John Burns
—like other really successful men—believed in himself.
There was no false humility and self-depreciation about
the man; he could say—what every action of the
man indicates—"Whatever I have done, I have never

shown the white feather." That is something of the spirit which makes for success: Faith in Self, Industry, and Courage to do the right.

Do not look too high and neglect the present—what can be done now. Everything depends on your ability to deal with the *now*, the to-day possibilities or opportunities, and turn them to the best account. That is the best way to get to the top of the ladder in the near future.

The struggle to make headway in life is no more difficult now than it has always been. Success came to the industrious then, and it will come to them now. Adopt similar methods, and adapt—*i.e.* educate—yourself for the work in hand. Old methods are dying out, and the burden of life is increasingly great for the unskilled, but not for the industrious and skilled. Out of a thousand young men who start in life, probably only one is an all-round success. What of the others? The bulk of them go into whatever was handiest, regardless of their adaptability. They are square men in round holes, and were never either at home or interested in their work or themselves. Some of these might have made headway and adapted or educated themselves to be of use—cigars, billiards, courting and what not filled in their spare time, to their disadvantage. They lived in " Micawber land," and looked forward to luck, influence, opportunity, or for " something to turn up," while neglecting the present. These are among the failures. Others get into a *rut*, and having no initiative, go, or grit, manage to jog along in that rut as

passable employees, never likely to come to anything
or make any advance. A small minority having go,
industry, and the wisdom to see that success does not
depend on luck, a university education, on "Influence"
—with the capital " I "—they wasted no time in dreaming, sleeping, and loafing till opportunity turned up,
or until luck was measured out to them by fickle
fortune; they seized time by the forelock, and by
application to that which was nearest at hand, in the
sphere most required, worked, planned, and turned up
or found opportunities for themselves. One out of
these became a captain of industry, a leader, expert,
an employer, an example, a master and a man, one
among men worthy of note and imitation. Rest
assured it is not the men who have had lucky starts,
influence, and all that who have made the most of
life, but those who—without these advantages—have
Faith in Themselves, and out of these, with limited
capital wisely employed, have made the greatest
successes in life. What these have done it is yours
to do—according to age, fitness, determination, and
perseverance. Have Faith in Yourself, and steadily,
hail, rain, or shine, work up to your standard.

We know of not a few who have lost "heart"
because of some external reversion in their affairs
over which they had no control. Some of these have
looked and looked again at their trouble, until fasci-
nated and held in thrall. A threepenny bit held
between the eye and the sun will be large enough
to obscure its brilliancy, and to blot out the beauties

of the surrounding scenery, made charmingly attractive by radiant beams which give light and warmth to the whole. Equally, small troubles as well as large ones, if held close enough to the mental vision, obscure the light from the mind, and keep the blinded one —although self-blinded—from seeing opportunities, methods, and ways of retrieving lost fortunes.

Many excuses are made for folding the arms, "throwing up the sponge"—ill-health, old age, uncertainties, and mostly "fear of a fear" that they will not be successful. That "fear of a fear" is the bedrock psychological obstacle, *within* which is the real cause of losing heart and giving up, instead of recommencing the battle of life again, like a sensible man.

The doyen of the medical profession in Glasgow, through the failure of the Glasgow City Bank, was rendered penniless at sixty-five years of age. He was a shareholder in the unlimited liability concern. Everything was swept away, through no fault of his own. He did not sit down and cry over it. He had two valuable assets, *character* and *ability*, *i.e.* Self-reliance. To-day, as I write this, Dr Burns is ninety-five, surrounded by every comfort, the materialised fruitage of his ability, and more than ever esteemed by his medical confrères, old patients, and the public, and his intimates, for his character and sterling worth. It is not money, it is character which makes for success; and money without character means the worst kind of failure: moral degeneracy, vulgarity, with ostentation, whether the individual moves in Society, with the capital "S," or in other ranks without the "S."

I have known many other men who, through financial crashes, went down, and many others, equally badly hit, who rose again, not because of the possession of " means," but from the possession of character and ability—the first being an asset which in due course commanded " means," influence, and credit; and the second consisting of a knowledge of their own powers, grit, self-reliance, hopefulness, and steady perseverance.

Do not get down-hearted because of reverses, the loss of a situation, or other circumstances. If you cannot fight your battle on one line, turn about and fight it out on another. If one door closes, look for the opening of another, or, better still, open one. It may take years to build up a reputation—character and ability,—but with it you can face adverse circumstances, and eventually turn them to account.

We owe the Waverley Novels to the financial crash of an eminent printing firm, still in existence. That is an object-lesson. Reverse tested the character and ability of Sir Walter Scott. We know the result. Poverty proved a stimulus to the sluggish temperament of Goldsmith, and to it we owe the charming story, *The Vicar of Wakefield*. Necessity has its virtues. Thackeray would not have given us *Vanity Fair*, had it not been for necessity which compelled application. Money does not make either genius or character, but is often the means of concealing, and the lack of it instrumental in revealing, both.

It is quite possible you may say, "What has this to do with me? I do not claim to be a genius." Possibly not, but you no doubt claim to be a man. Well, the most valued possession of a man is character. You are making it every day. It will stand you in good stead in the dark hours, when dark hours come, as they do come in the lives of most men. Character is like a diamond, it shines best in the dark, i.e. adversity.

The Scottish banks, next to the Civil Service, present admirable openings for young men who mean to get on in life. The positions will compare favourably with clerkships in modern commerce, and the position of salesmen in houses of repute. The salaries may be like the hours, somewhat short to commence. There is the advantage of systematic training, certain promotion—for all the highest posts in the banking system are held by those who were once boys, who entered at ten pounds per annum years ago. Should the bank clerk, agent, or manager retire through age limit, he has a retiring allowance which will compare favourably with that of the Civil Service. Who are the men to succeed? Those who come in at the first and apply themselves to the work in hand, and fit themselves, with cheerful courage, for their work, and are consequently ready for responsibilities and promotion when opportunities come.

It is always the same story—success comes to those who look and work for it. But it is not in banking or in the Civil Service—by which I mean the permanent official staff of the country, from telegraph boy to permanent secretary of the Treasury—but in the larger world of commerce, science, art, and the professions, that the greatest rewards of trust in self and earnest endeavour are to be obtained. The workers get the prizes, not the drones. The man who takes himself well in hand, is the man to succeed.

Cultivate Personal Magnetism. Be healthy, clean, vigorous, prompt, orderly, and act like a man who means to succeed: confidence begets confidence. Place yourself in the way of attainment by making yourself thorough master of whatever you are employed at. Curb your tongue, master your temper, be prompt and willing. Create a name for promptitude, attention, and civility; these qualities are in demand and have a commercial value. Think of yourself as courageous, reliable, steady, and persevering. Don't bother about luck, influence, and matters of that sort; just make up your mind that you are going to be a more thorough, steady, painstaking, courteous employee than ever. Treasure every feature which you know to be good in yourself, and make up your mind you are going to inprove on that. Don't worry about failures and defects, for it is a mistake and a waste of time to do that, but just keep the good in view. Cultivate Personal Magnetism, which means manliness, Self-reliance, and a healthy, bright, plucky spirit.

Think these matters over in the quiet privacy of your heart. "Say nothing to anybody" about it; you will make most headway thus. Thus, too, you will prepare yourself to take practical lessons in self-culture later on. Meanwhile, get a good hold upon yourself; "believe in yourself"; hold yourself in honourable estimation in your own mind—as worthy of respect—and keep yourself there; exercise your best thoughts and endeavours; in that way you will do the best for all that is best in you. The things which are weak and faulty will become less and less conspicuous, and you yourself, by your own determination, more and more fit.

CHAPTER IV

PERSONAL MAGNETISM AND SELF-CULTURE—*continued*

"Never assent merely to please others, for that is, besides Flattery, oftentimes Untruth ; and discovers a Mind liable to be servile and base. Nor contradict to vex others, for that shows ill temper and provokes, but profits no Body."—WILLIAM PENN.

THIS is an age of enterprise, and old-fashioned methods —whether in shipping or shopkeeping, mechanics or chemistry, lecturing or preaching—mean stagnation. To be conservative and not move with the requirements of the times means, if not complete, comparative failure. Superior combination, methods of organisation, mean increased prosperity ; and neglect, or contentment with the more easy-going methods of three or four decades ago, which suited our fathers, foreordains obliteration in these days of keen competition. Up-to-date methods are demanded. While this is so, the essential qualities which were the backbone of the old-fashioned methods, remain still the essential factors of success in all departments of public and private enterprises to-day. These qualities are Self-reliance, Personal Magnetism, integrity, reliability, method, order, ability and tact. If the longer hours and the more easy-going style have vanished, and keener competition has demanded higher education, technical knowledge, and labour-saving appliances in workshop and office, the man of character is more than ever in demand. The man who is most in demand in all departments is the man who creates that demand by his Self-reliance. He does not wait till the world finds him out; he does not simply pull down the shutters and wait for customers to come along and patronise him. He goes into the highways and by-ways, and by up-to-date methods of advertisement, by mail department, aided thereto by travellers, specialists, courteous and attentive servants, compels the public to see and get his goods. Promptitude, good faith, reliability, " stuff up to sample," " value for cash " or its commercial equivalent, complete the bargain. The public realise that the head of that firm is in his office studying its wants, and can supply them. The confidence of the public grows and the firm prospers, because its brains — directors and managers — have determined that it shall prosper. The head of each department is picked out for the post on account of his fitness. He has been trained and grown in the business. Thousands have been, too; but these men have shown special grit, fitness, and they have been selected as self-reliant, reliable, thorough men.

The firm that deals unfairly—substitute lawyer, bank agent, stockbroker, general dealer, manufacturer, or yourself for firm—goes to the wall eventually. It may be safely said that enterprise—which means square dealing with promptitude, conducted on Self-reliance principles—spells success.

Governments, educational institutes, or commercial houses cannot be better than their component parts, duly organised, make them ; and that organising is and must be the result of some leading and dominating mind. The possessor of that mind will have either forced his way to the front through his manifest abilities, or he will have been selected because of them as the most suitable man for the post. Whoever he is, he will be the best, most self-reliant, and capable man his party, department, or firm can get hold of. He has generally commenced at the beginning, become familiar with all details, and studied the demands of the public. In addition to this, he has probably in a measure created those demands by his methods of procedure. This man, whoever he may be, understands himself, and knows his worth, his people, pupils, public, and his firm's requirements. He gathers up the threads and thrumbs of information and utilizes these to the best advantage. Being thorough, go-ahead, and enthusiastic himself, he infuses these qualities into those about him. By his character and abilities he has created a demand for himself—as manager, partner, leader, or proprietor. By Faith in Self, he has created a demand for himself. By his Self-reliance he begets confidence. The people love strength and admire enterprise, and the man having these qualities obtains their support. He creates success for his firm, and position and honour for himself.

The prime mover of the wheels of success is always an active, wide-awake man—one who puts thought into his work. Possibly he was only a clerk the other day, manager of a department but yesterday, and becomes head of the firm to-day. We inquire into his history and find that he has not been a rolling-stone. He has been in the firm twelve, fifteen, twenty-five years, and he has made headway while brighter and, at times, more promising men have stuck in some rut or have left. To what do we attribute his success? Influence, so-called? Not a bit of it. Luck or love? No. Self-reliance, which exhibited itself in attention to details, industry, and steadiness, plus the ability of assimilating new ideas and applying them. Your shivering, grumbling clerk-drudge who has no faith in himself, and mechanically gets through his routine work, with no interest, on a pound or thirty shillings a week, has no chance for such promotion. But your magnetic, self-reliant, ready to learn, not afraid to work, wide-awake, decent tongued, suitably dressed, prompt and courteous youth, gets the promotion. He has what is called Personal Magnetism. He attracts attention, and reaps the reward.

When our American cousins speak of a magnetic personality, or Personal Magnetism, they mean that undefinable attractiveness by which they are drawn to a healthy, vigorous, self-reliant, tactful person. The strong, healthy-minded man, who is tactful, agreeable— but not weak—is a magnetic person. He is strong, reliable, and attracts, not by posing, good looks, twirling his moustache or cane, but by healthy manliness graced by tact and courtesy—is strong and agreeable without any make-believe.   Sound health, Self-reliance, definite ideas that lead, and tact, are summed up in the term Personal Magnetism.   Self-reliance is the iron ; Personal Magnetism is the glove of the successful man. To be agreeable, cultivate tact ; a magnetic man is not only manly, he is also tactful.

One element in success is tactfulness.   Tact can be employed in business concerns just as well as in private intercourse.   And just a word in passing— tact is a factor in agreeableness, therefore a feature in Personal Magnetism, and there is no reason why woman should have a monopoly of the grace of courtesy.   Tact, originally and physically signifying touch, applied mentally, signifies nice perception of our fellows conjoined to an intuitive power of appreciating the position and doing what is necessary in a refined, considerate way ; adapting one's speech and behaviour to the circumstances ; in a word, courtesy allied to intuition and judgment.   Such is tact plainly defined.   We can the better appreciate what it is—to employ or attempt a bull—when it is absent.   The want of a little tact has been a fertile source of failure in business relations, in domestic affairs, in those affairs, too, when the young man's fancy lightly turns to love.   A bull in a china-shop will create less havoc than the tactless man with customers, pupils, or affairs of the heart.   The tactless man generally does the wrong thing at the right time— another paradox — or the right thing in a wrong manner, which invites rejection or resentment.   Perceiving something wrong, explanations only make confusion worse confounded, and leave nothing lacking in the way of either insolence or stupidity. The tactful person, allowing for the personal peculiarities of those about him, will, without abating one jot or tittle of either honesty or manly worth, quietly study to place each person at their ease; will listen with interest to what they have to say, make their happiness his own; give consolation where it is required, just by being simply considerate, patient, discriminating, and genial.

To be tactful is not a difficult matter; a beginning can be easily made by a little repression of oneself— self-conscious assurance of one's importance—and the employment of courtesy, with a few genial smiles thrown in, and being mindful of the occasions when, though speech may be silvern, silence is golden. In this way one puts himself in the shoes of his clients and friends, and thinks of their way of looking at things and of their requirements. There is something in this of doing unto others as you would have them do to you. Never mind whether they rise to your wishes or not, make it a practice to practise tact on all occasions. If a person grunts and groans about his misfortunes, bad-luck, or ill-health, there is no need to make him feel how little these things interest you. And there is less need in waiting breathlessly to jump in and retail yours. You can show kindly sympathy without encouraging their state of mind, and when possible, and without aggressiveness, lead them to take a more hopeful view of things. It will not only do them more good, but will make them *feel good*, *i.e.* better for having their talk with you. Not so much because you talked to them, but because of your evident interest in them, shown by allowing them to make you an agreeable "Father Confessor." A tactful man is a good listener, and when he speaks he says nothing he will regret having attributed to him, even though it does not lose anything by waiting or in the carrying. The chief quality in a tactful person is discreet silence: the wisdom to know when to keep the mouth shut and yet not appear to do it: to avoid the personal in speaking, and in all cases to avoid the disagreeable. The tactful person never interrupts the conversation of others by rushing in with his opinions on all sorts of subjects, either to air himself or his "knowledge of quotations"; much less will he take up the running when "male gossips" are flaying some fellow-mortal. Life is too real and earnest for that. The man of tact does not talk about himself or his own troubles, and when a subject is under consideration he allows others to have their say while he discriminates—no two persons think alike. Where he does not approve, he is silent; where it is absolutely necessary to state his opinion—if he has a real opinion to state—he does it in a way which disarms antagonism. He leads, but does not attempt to drive. He has faith in himself; but he does not wear his heart upon his sleeve, much less will he proclaim that fact to others. A tactful man is a welcome man. He oils the machinery of a business house; his office work is conducted with a minimum of friction; as a strong, self-reliant man his society is courted, and he is welcome everywhere, where that welcome is worth, simply because *he has learnt how to be silent and to do it gracefully.* That is tact.

The tactful man is a shrewd judge of human nature, endowed with the grace of humour, with sense not to take his fun at the cost of another's feelings. His mirth is contagious and does not bite. No one is made uneasy because of his presence, behaviour, or conversation. You do not creep into your shell because he approaches. You reserve your vacant laugh and smile of vacuity for another occasion, because you respect the tactful man, as well as enjoy and welcome his presence. It is not what he does so much as the way he does it; it is not so much what he says, as the manner of saying it. But it will be noticed what he says is something useful, beneficial and pleasant, and the manner of saying is free and unrestrained, lacking the suspicion of self-consciousness. He is self-possessed and self-controlled, and whatever of Self-reliance the man possesses, the personal pronoun is not either conspicuous or underlined in his conversation. It is *you* he appears interested in, not himself. He may not be a Christian professor, but he will be a good Christian all the same, because he can weep with those who weep and rejoice with those who rejoice. If he helps the widows in their distress, or uses the leverage of his influence to help the orphan, he does not buttonhole you and proclaim that so-and-so is a pensioner of his, and enumerate the good he has done and is doing.

You can learn something of tactfulness by putting *self* in the background, neither explaining, defending, nor advocating yourself; by avoiding undue criticism and fault-finding. Leave grumbling to those who find nothing better to do, and who are unable to place a higher estimate on self. *Feel agreeable and be it.* Practise being agreeable in little things, and an urbane, gracious, considerate manner — which need not be servile—will become second nature. Even though you know those about you may be lacking in essential manly virtues, and probably possess faults too numerous to be conveniently catalogued much less to make pleasant reading, they must nevertheless be very poor specimens of humanity if they do not possess some good qualities. Never mind their faults; look for and manage tactfully to draw out their good qualities. Failings are always easy enough to find. Possibly no pains have been taken to conceal things men sometimes boast about, and which bring them little credit. It is nearly as bad as boasting about talents, gifts, and other qualities, for which some fish for compliments and admiration. Boasting in either case is a sign of weakness. Be considerate anyway; no two are alike. Possibly behind and underneath all this childishness of manhood—boastfulness and its associating vice and tyranny, peculiar to the bully—there may be, in fact must be, good qualities. Look for these. *No human being is wholly bad.* Tact has something of the milk of human kindness in it. It is not always in the robes of a judge; it is an advocate, restrained, thoughtful, and kind. Cultivate and make a practice of studying character, not to prose about the faults but to find the good of others; strive to understand the feelings, sentiments, desires, and motives of your fellows; see how far you can sympathise instead of being antagonistic ; when you don't know the whole truth, avoid thinking the worst. Cultivate kindness, benevolence, and sympathy in yourself, and you will somehow draw out the best qualities in others.

Tact is the power by which we place ourselves most sympathetically in *touch* with our fellows, and draw out and perchance lead them to do their best. The tactful man succeeds where the tactless blunder, bounce, and *fail*. Tact is a factor in Personal Magnetism. Cultivate it.

You can learn by example the best course to adopt and what to avoid. You will do well to exercise tact while in the company of persons who take pleasure in meanness and uncharitableness. No need to argue, much less defend yourself. When you cannot adroitly change the subject of rejoicing in the discovery of other men's faults, take refuge in silence or in smiles—or both. The tactful man, however, will find some way out. It will be by repression more than expression: by turning the topic, or dexterously calling attention to the time or the scenery; or, if in business, to the work in hand and in which he may have or should have an interest. Tact is civility plus common-

sense.　Tact is the great outstanding feature of Personal
Magnetism.

Reading man's constitution aright, it is clear that
man was made for happiness—to enjoy life and give joy.
Cheerfulness not only promotes health in the possessor,
but gives pleasure and happiness to others.　It is
not only an attractive, but a health-promoting force.
Philosophers and poets have in prose and poetry sung
its praises, and the homely adage, " Laugh and be well,"
has been coined out of shrewd observation of the facts.
It is a duty we owe to ourselves to cultivate cheerfulness.　Thomas Carlyle, the seer of Chelsea, who knew
something of both melancholy and cheerfulness, said:
" Wondrous is the strength of cheerfulness, altogether
past calculation its powers of endurance.　Efforts to be
permanently useful must be uniformly joyous, a spirit
all sunshine, graceful from very gladness, beautiful
because bright."　Cheerfulness is not only a safeguard
of health and a promoter of it, but a psychological
foundation for it.　It is a magnetic health builder,
within our power to consciously and deliberately
employ with advantage.

If you want to be a magnetic personality, think,
grow, and live cheerfully.　You may have the integrity
of a saint, the intellect of a double-first and a senior
wrangler to boot, and in personal appearance equal to
Apollo Belvidere for handsomeness; but without the
humanising and sympathetic sweetness of cheerfulness,
all the foregoing advantages count for little.　On the
other hand your intelligence may lack the polish of the

schools, and in appearance you may be as plain as a hand-rail, but the earnest, sterling character and moral worth, which causes "the face to shine," will render you welcome to man, woman, and child. Cultivate cheerfulness for its own sake, for your own sake, and you will be a healthy, attractive, and welcomed person.

Cheerfulness, like health, is a natural endowment, but it can be cultivated. However you feel, don't go through life with a downcast head, a hanging lip, with your mouth down at the corners. Fish for sympathy and get kicked! Hold your head up; put the best face on matters. You have no right to bother others with your troubles—real or imaginary. Look happy, cheerful, and successful. Keep your own counsel, and you will pull through every time. You will see things in a better light, and tackle problems with a clearer brain. The quiet, complacent, magnetic eye arrests attention, begets confidence, and, whether master or man, will materially facilitate your success in life.

Thackeray, the novelist, was quite right when he compared the world to a looking glass. If you frown and scowl at it, you will receive a frown and a scowl in return. If you are pleasant and cheerful, it will reflect these qualities and you will have little to grumble about. Next to cheerfulness, appearance is a good asset in success. A very ordinary face can be illuminated by intelligence and the self-reliant stamp of Personal Magnetism. The tawdry, careless man has no self-respect, and without that there is no Self-reliance. In whatever position of life it may be yours to fill or to make, have regard to your appearance. "Create the best impression you can, and as fast as you can, by a proper care of your person, dress, and manners. In business, people often have to judge hastily. They give those who favourably impress them at a glance the first chance. Well, it's a thing to aim at getting. Can you afford to throw it away?" was the advice of the late Mr Peabody, the well-known philanthropist and millionaire.

It is important to create good impressions. Whatever you may be—soldier or civilian, professional man —of which there are innumerable varieties—chemist, medical man, lawyer, accountant, civil engineer, architect, banker, bank agent, insurance agent, superintendent, clerk, salesman, engineer, mechanic,—make a point of dressing to suit the nature of your work, and in private in accordance with your position, and at all times neatly, orderly, and tastefully. Manners and appearance reflect habits. Rightly or wrongly, you will at first sight be estimated by your appearance, manner, and the impressions which these create. No man can hope to get on in the world who neglects attention to those little details of spruceness, neatness, order, courtesy, and urbanity, which are as needful as purity, honesty, perseverance, in demonstrating one's faith in Self, Self-reliance, and determination to make headway in life.

There is no doubt that as long as human nature is creeping up to perfection, there will be double-dealers, shufflers, and cranks among the "smart set of hustlers after money." There is no need to look up the betting news, and racing tips, or the sequels demonstrated in the Police and Session Courts, and reported in the daily press, for examples. Everyone has a bit of imperfection in him, and on that bit the wise man keeps his finger. Even from a selfish point of view, "Honesty is the best policy." It is productive of fewer regrets, and no real ones. Imperfect as we may be, there is in the most imperfect a love of honesty, straight dealing, and fair play ; an admiration for that strength which integrity exhibits in others—even when not possessed by the admirer. "His word is as good as his bond," is a certificate of character, beyond price and priceless in any sphere of life, an asset which any good-going bank will advance cash on. The man who has this reputation need not dread difficulty in getting out of the complications which a financial crisis or bad trade brings. Straight dealing pays ; it is one of the soundest and cheapest methods of advertising and building up business. We all know of professions, businesses, and individuals wrecked because of the lack of that intrinsic element—honesty. One of the very best impressions we can make on our clients and customers is that which comes with the clear gaze, backed by a conscientious conviction of square dealing. That kind of Self-reliance impresses one, without words. When words are required, it gives them the right ring—finds its harmonious response in that which is best in those who trust us.

The world has need of you, and the best that is in you. Look it out. Put yourself in the way of attainment. Don't wait till the world finds you out and covets your best gifts. Covet the best gifts yourself, and make the best of yourself, and your value will be certain of appreciation. Never mind the mistakes of the past, and sit—like many fools—among the ruins of the great might-have-been's, making yourself more sore and useless by scratching the boils of disappointment with the potsherds of " bad luck." Banish care and worry, by present healthy occupation.

By all means let the past go. Think what is best to be done now. Go into your closet and think. Your closet may be a room, or the middle of a field—it matters not—be alone. Go and think. Take counsel with yourself. Thinking is good for one. There is far too much gush, shout, and self-advertisement and too many hollow performances in the world to-day—for want of good thinking. Think out ways and means. Think out what is best ; what you want to attain, aye, and what you want to get rid of, and you will start aright, for Personal Magnetism, Will-power, and Success.

Never mind the other man or that woman. *It is yourself with whom you have to deal.* Put yourself right and begin at the beginning. Put yourself in the witness box of your present attainments and of your past experience. Take the good in you for granted. Also take it for granted that you have not made one tithe the use of it which you should have done. It is well to start with broad principles, and one is, "There is more good in a man than evil." Then make up your mind to find out that good and make the most of it. Another is, "There is more which makes for Health than Disease in the organisation." Health is yours, then. Keep what you have and get more by the way of moderation, temperance, work, or exercise, or a more hygienic life. Another principle is, "If you have got health enough to get over the shock of your birth, you will have enough to get over many other shocks." This vitality is to be conserved and maintained, and longevity, with a healthy old age to boot, is yours. And the last is, and this is the greatest of all—"Mind governs matter." It is as imminent in the human organisation as the Eternal One is in Creation. See that you make this principle a fact in consciousness, THAT YOUR MIND GOVERNS. You have had difficulties in the past, may have in the future, and in your new career get some hard knocks. Take them; come up smiling every time. Hard knocks are good. Trouble precedes rejoicing; preparation, success. Make a point to be cheerful, and you will have health, happiness, and the joy of living, because you are beginning at the beginning and putting yourself in the way of attainment of that which is to be prized—A SANE AND HEALTHY MANHOOD.

The man who lives with moral courage in this world fears no man here, and need fear none hereafter. A straight life to-day is the best preparation for to-morrow, or for that life which succeeds all to-morrows.

Anyway, live your best life to-day. And smile and work, and work and smile.

Benjamin Franklin in *Poor Richard's Almanack* wrote : "God helps them that help themselves," and among other things, "Honesty is the best policy." And with these keys played the manly tune of a real sound life. For this world gave us these healthy keys to play an honest and entrancing tune for ourselves. Energy, shrewdness, clean-mindedness, moral courage, and a healthy enthusiasm, are the instruments with which you may play the game too.

SUCCESS IN LIFE IS YOURS, IF YOU WILL HAVE IT.

YOU WERE MADE TO BE HEALTHY. WHY NOT BE ?

OTHERS HAVE BEEN SUCCESSFUL. WHY NOT YOU ?

IN ALL TIMES AND NOW, THERE HAVE BEEN THE GREAT AND GOOD AND THE MAGNETIC. WHY SHOULD YOU FAIL ?

WHAT ONE MAN CAN DO, ANOTHER MAY. WHY SHOULD NOT YOU BE EQUALLY SUCCESSFUL ?

You are nearest to yourself. You will be closest at hand to help yourself. And SELF-HELP is the GREATEST OF ALL HELP. Let it be yours to render yourself cheerful assistance. You have got it in you and you can do it.

When you read this lesson, think over it. Pick out that which is most suitable, and for practice find time for half an hour's quiet thinking. Think over the day that has gone. Have you learned or done anything worth remembering ? Is it worth repeating or following up ? Don't despise routine work, little details. The man that keeps his buttons bright is generally able to give a good account of himself in the field. What mistakes have you made in work, temper, judgment, or conduct which it will be better to avoid in the future? In the quiet calm of reflection you will learn to put greater energy into what is best, and also exercise greater determination to avoid what is least desirable. When responsibility is thrown upon you, do not fear to accept, and if it is not, PREPARE FOR IT AND LOOK FORWARD TO DISCHARGE IT SUCCESSFULLY.

CHAPTER V

SUCCESS AND SOME METHODS OF ITS ATTAINMENT

" We are not sent into this world to do anything into which we cannot put our hearts. We have certain work to do for our bread, and that is to be done strenuously ; other work to do for our delight, and that is to be done heartily—neither is to be done by halves or shifts, but with a will, and what is not worth this effort is not to be done at all."—Ruskin.

A few moments may be given to the consideration of what Success is and what it is not. And then to a few practical hints towards Success through Self-help.

If Success merely means the obtaining of money, position, and the gratification of the intellect and the appetite at the sacrifice of the higher qualities which distinguish the man from the animal, and also the material delights of the former in housing, clothing, feeding, and gross instincts of self-preservation on the material plane at the cost of true health and manhood, it is too dear at the price. Yet how frequently a man's success in life is gauged by these three things— money, position, and the power of self-gratification— without regard to those humanising, lofty, noble, and true qualities which really make for Success. A life which sweetens, uplifts, cheers, and comforts his world by the living in it, leaves a memory full of all that is manly and sound behind to comfort and cheer still.

Success of this kind is too much overlooked by many, in their desire to attain wealth and position. Not that wealth and position are undesirable. The greater one's real attainments and the more influential the position, certainly the more power one has to do good or ill. Wealth, position, intellectual genius, much less plodding and industrious talent, are not to be despised, simply because some have attained these—in greater or less measure—and have either turned them to ignoble uses, or have left them unemployed, save for such purposes as living a life wholly self-centred in eating, drinking, and indulging the latest fashions in frock-coats and ties; to say nothing of their meanness of conception as to the real purpose of life, and only because they have a little more money, one or two more rooms in their villas, and an acre or two more shooting in their estates than others. This may be called Success, but it is not.

The hustle and rush, the gambling spirit on exchange, in the commercial marts, which invade all grades of society, in the hope of getting something for nothing at the expense of their fellows, and which very often does, is not Success. It may give wealth and position, and these constitute the very essence of failure. Every medical man knows, as I know, that these successes, aye, and failures too, are the parents of a thousand ills, nerve wrecks, moral disasters, mental unbalancing, suicidal mania, and possibly worse. Quietness is a

pleasure unknown; home life a secondary consideration; intellectual and helpful conversations, these are
unknown, as there is little to talk about save the last
successful (?) deal, the odds that did the trick, the
last "attachment," and even too much hurry for these,
and too much fear lest the other fellow should get to
know too much. This kind of Success—mere wealth-
getting at the cost of that which is best in manhood;
the kind of Success which appeals most to those enamoured in brokers' boys who became millionaires, and
held the railways, mines, in the hollow of their hands,
or who "cornered" the world's cotton or wheat—is
not the Success which these instructions advocate.

Without being enamoured by the princes of Pluto-
cracy, there are many esteemed successful men who
never wasted an hour or a minute which could be
turned into money. They have made the money, and
are looked up to as successful men in their particular
walk in life, whatever that may be. They may be
esteemed public-spirited men, whose voice and influence in political and religious affairs are worthy of
example, and yet, if we penetrate below the surface,
and confess what we learn—their success must be
acknowledged to be the blankest of failures. They
have sacrificed health, and the joy of life, to money-
making; they have starved their intellect of wholesome culture; wife and children have been neglected—
not deprived of material needs of life, but of wholesome
love, companionship, and healthy support. Excitement,
entertainments, travel, rush, show, and selfish indiffer-

ence to their fellow-creatures' woes, and a miserable egotism for the admiration of the public, have taken the place of a well-balanced, self-contained happiness, which is the legitimate finish of true Success.

While all this is true, there are no real reasons why money should not be made, because there have been moral failures among the wealthy, and animalism—gilded or naked—has been shamelessly enthroned by them. We do not need to go among the " success-ful" ones of the earth for this triumph of the pro-pensities. The possession or the want of wealth, or a fair share of the material means of life, is no indication of the want of morals, manhood, character, and ability.

Real Success is proportionate to the possession of Self-reliance, true self-control or balance. Health and happiness are to be found with these—that is to say, real Success in life. Such Success is not measured on the terms which represent money, in copper and railway shares, house property, bonds or deposit receipts; but it may be compatible with humble enough positions, a limited cupboard, and a straightened purse.

Success lies in making the most of oneself; taking advantage of opportunities ; fitting oneself to environ-ment; and in the culture of self so as to improve one's possessions. And while increased means are secured by greater initiative, industry, and application, they have been secured *by the advancement of what is best in us,* and not by its degradation, and a petrifaction of feeling or sensitiveness to the allurements of wealth and position merely.

The Success in life which means the absence of
restful, wholesome culture, domestic peace, the cheerful fireside, the kindly exchange of thought, the brightness of music, the joyous lifting of the voice in song or
hymn, the pleasure of playful wit, and the saving grace
of humour, is a sordid " success," which makes a " muck
rake " of a man—and at the cost of all that is manly.

Success based on the unfolding of whatever is best in
a man is the prize that is worth striving for.   It is a
success based on the knowledge of self, on a consciousness of one's weaknesses, and a greater consciousness
of one's powers of mastery.   None are perfect in this
world.   Although we are not " fallen angels," we are
more or less ascending reptiles, no longer eating of the
dust and crawling on our bellies, but raised to the
upright, with our heads towards heaven and our feet
upon the rock of human consciousness—a living soul.
There is a trace of the reptile and the monkey in us
yet, and it has brought with it the crawling posture and
thievish tricks which our barbaric forebears possessed,
with their lust of possession, of blood and strength.   We
know this, but it is not all of us.   By no means is it
all; there is the power of the spirit, the finer forces of
the soul, and a brain and organisation, fit instruments
for the manifestation of our highest sentiments—moral
and spiritual faculties, which ever differentiate the man
from the brute.

Success means not the elimination of the brute or
the emasculation of one single atom of those physical
powers which make for virile manhood or prowess ; nor

yet the loss of brawn and muscle, which our cave-dwelling prehistoric forefathers possessed, and we in a measure retain; but the mastery of these invaluable possessions and their subordination to the control of an enlightened intellect, which is the true will.

Success means that we have learned to subordinate our feelings and emotions to the position of servants, whose joy it is to obey our will; it means the greater play of the moral and spiritual powers; and it means the control and direction of the will. Yes, it means more than all this; it means we have more truly discovered ourselves. The crude, outward, external consciousness of life—which shallowly and superficially estimates our fellows by their failures and animality, and indeed ourselves by no very exalted standard of experience—gives place to a higher consciousness of worth, of the possibilities of intellectual, spiritual, and moral unfoldment; and, finally, to a knowledge that, apart from the ordinary powers of the mind as revealed to ordinary consciousness, we possess more subtile subconscious and psychical powers, which we can call into play to develop that which is best in us.

If, ignorantly, we have been limited in the knowledge of self, and only judged of our fellows and ourselves by appearances, our judgment has been unrighteous, pessimistic, and unworthy, not only to ourselves, but also to our fellows. We have been hypnotising ourselves to failure. It is the purpose of these lessons that you may, by gradual steps, make yourself a success in life, through an increased knowledge of yourself, and the cultivation of Self-reliance and all which that means.

Success does not mean the possession of wealth, position, and public applause or envy. It means the possession of self.

For a little we must still generalise, and then travel from the general to the particular—from theory to practice. All in good time. Don't worry; don't hurry; but, whatever you do, don't loaf. And whatever you are doing, concentrate and give your attention to that, and you will have the pleasure to realize it will be all the better done in consequence.

Don't worry. What? You have a lot to worry about. Yes, I understand. I have been there. We make one-fourth of our worries by being in a hurry, and manufacture most of the rest by dwelling on these, when the mind should be directed into wiser and healthier channels.

Work worries; pace kills the unsuccessful man. Work is distasteful. He prefers to kill time; is more anxious about holidays, and getting out of work, than giving his time to it while at it. Then he wonders why he is not successful. You will concentrate your mind on that which you love. There is often more nerve exhaustion caused by one week's holidays than by six months' work. This is where the *pace* kills. You will not concentrate where there is lack of interest. Where you are really interested there will be no trouble either to concentrate or to work. Every position in life has its drawbacks. But these are not reasons why we should not make the best of life or work, love or duty or care. It is quite possible to make the best of life and all things—no matter how we are situated. Next to worrying about the past and one's failures therein, there is another equally stupid and foolish waste of nerve and mental energy— worrying about the future. Please don't. It is both idle and stupid. The dread of the unknown is to be avoided. Do your best now. What? You might fail. Never mind that. Do your best now. You cannot commence sooner. Trust God. Trust yourself. Have faith in yourself. Leave the future alone. Don't paralyse your vision of the present, and your ability to think and work in the present, by dreading what the future has or may never have in store for you.

You are a disappointed man? Somehow things go wrong. You are not alone in these experiences. Let disappointment be taken as a stimulant to greater effort, and never allow it to act as a discouragement. You have made mistakes in the past? You have done some sowing, and will have some reaping to do. Well, do it. Face the music like a man. Don't shift the responsibility on to anyone else, even in thought. Stand to it, and you will be all the better. Anyway, your life work, so far, cannot be wholly wrong, and there will be something good to reap as well. That will be good and helpful, not only for yourself, but for others who will share the benefit. That will be good. Anyway, take the consequences like a man; yourself and the world will be all the better for it. We are all learning. You could not think, ten years ago, with the head and the experiences you have now. There is something in that. It is worth thinking about. Start afresh, and throw away all gloom, misery, fear of failure, worry—present and future—and then you will be in the right spirit to be benefited and helped by the Spirit of Manhood and Experience that dictates these lessons of Self-help. Don't fear failure. Failure only comes to those who seek it, drift into it, and otherwise hypnotise themselves into it.

All this talk about failure and not getting on in life, want of interest and ill-luck, and the rest of it, although as old as the hills, is a weak and very unmanly cry. If you are guilty of it, have done with it for ever. At any rate you are only telling your listeners what an idiot, or worse, you have been.

"The world seems overstocked with everything," said one of those self-made failures in the gloomiest tones of the oh-do-please-pity-me-kind to Lord Palmerston. "I can tell you some things that the world has never enough of," replied Lord Palmerston, "and that it is always willing to pay for—intelligence, honesty, courage, and perseverance. In these the supply will never exceed the demand."

There is a ready market for your courage, honesty, intelligence, and perseverance at the present moment. Whatever you can excel in ; whatever your sphere in life, these qualifications will help you to make the best of both.

Wherever your interest lies, there you will concen-

trate your energies.   You cannot do a thing well, if you
are thinking of somebody or something else.   Besides,
it is a foolish waste of energy.   I will refer to this
again.   Meanwhile pull yourself together and march
forward to the task before you.

I think you will accept these remarks as being
sensible and to the point.   Where you have failed, it
has been because you have lacked this spirit.   Your
attentions have been divided.   You have been attempting one thing while you have been thinking about
other matters.   Well, put all that away.   It can be
done.   Make up your mind to do it, and carry out not
only the foregoing suggestions, but also all those which
follow.

I want you to promise me in your mind two things :
(a) Prompt and Willing Obedience and
(b) SILENCE.

In asking Prompt and Willing Obedience, I promise
that I will not ask you to do anything which a man
cannot do, and certainly nothing which will not be of
decided advantage in the end.   If I should ask you, in
these lessons, to do something, the object of which you
may not understand at the time—DO IT.   All explanations will be given in due course.   But you get to work
and carry out directions.   Obey Orders as the next
best step to SUCCESS.   The FIRST STEP is to issue the
orders to yourself and see that they are obeyed.
Meanwhile obey mine.

The next thing I ask you to bear in mind is SILENCE.
There are few men in the world who have not a

companion or friend with whom they exchange thoughts more fully than with others. But, in this instance, these Instructions are *for you.* I enjoin secrecy, not because there is anything new, wonderful, or occult in these lessons, which I do not wish conveyed to others, except from myself; but I enjoin SILENCE, because of the benefits which will accrue to yourself. This will be made clearer as we proceed, and meanwhile, to simplify matters between us, and for your own benefit, the growth of your WILL-POWER and SELF-CONTROL, I ask two things as the foundation on which you are to build: OBEDIENCE and SILENCE. In other words, do what I tell you, and tell no one that you are doing so. It is not what a man says—" I am going to do, or I mean to do so and so,"—or what a man thinks about himself, or what he thinks others should think about him, that really tells in this best of all worlds to us now, BUT THAT WHICH HE DOES. THAT TELLS.

WORK, not WORDS. Ability to accomplish and the DOING OF IT speaks louder than words. Work demands respect, and, in its own department, WILL GET IT.

Possibly, at times, you are "short in the grain." Impulsive, too; ready to feel hurt or to give an impulsive answer when your projects do not meet with approval or you happen to be crossed. Here your offended Approbativeness would lead you to make bad, worse. Hence the necessity for Self-control, of which SILENCE is the truest expression. If your views are not accepted after they have been *respectfully* submitted, bow to the decision of your confrères or superiors, as the case may be. Consult them—quietly and respectfully—as to the course which they think it best for your discharge of duty. They will either ask for time, direct, or leave the matter for yourself. In the latter case, *accept the responsibility.* In any case, men must be won, not driven. Those who have a right to direct or command, must be allowed to do so. The man who pays the fiddler has a right to call the tune. *But that need not prevent the fiddler, when he sees a suitable opening, suggesting some new tunes, and thus gaining his point by the exercise of a little tact and patience.*

SILENCE and TACT will prove true friends. By the latter I do not mean sycophancy, but self-control and judgment amid all trials and difficulties. Respect for others and the exercising patience to listen to their ideas, will enable you by courteous ability to lead them to your own, when you have reason to believe your own are better. Those in command have power to issue orders. It is yours to obey. Theirs the responsibility for the orders. Yours the responsibility for the discharge of the duty or the seeing that the duty is discharged according to the position which you occupy. But, apart from all this, SILENCE and TACT are essential for the proper development of your own character. What you do, then, is for the best. You have an object in view : a laudable one—the bettering of your own conditions, and the further improvement of your own powers. By SILENCE YOU GAIN THE SELF-CONTROL AND THE FORCE OF CHARACTER YOU ADMIRE IN OTHERS,

AND YOU ARE ALSO ABLE TO CONCEAL DEFEAT, which may be yours at times. Gain power and conceal losses, and you achieve a reputation for ability and SUCCESS. You do more, you gain it.

By TACT, patient and courteous consideration of the views of others, you avoid raising obstacles—unnecessary obstacles—in your path to the goal which you have in view. Others may fuss, be impatient, irritable, and angry, even grossly offensive. Whatever the temptation, you be none of these things. Your quiet firmness will gain you greater ascendency and control. YOU HAVE IT IN YOU TO SUCCEED. This is the WAY, WALK YOU IN IT. I want you to believe in yourself; to have lofty and worthy ideals of what is manly, masterful, noble, and true, and—as far as you are able—to live up to these IDEALS. You have plenty of energy, and more staying power than you are aware of. You have latent potential forces as well as concentration of them to draw upon.

In the discharge of your duty or business, be quietly DIGNIFIED; ALWAYS ATTENTIVE, POLITE, AND PLEASANT-MANNERED. There is nothing like having a healthy, cheerful, and agreeable look, and live up to that and convince yourself of it. This will gain approval from superiors and the respect of inferiors, and, as a matter of fact, will draw people to you. They will open their minds to you; tell you of their affairs, solicit your counsel, or perhaps give you advice. You can use your own judgment as to your replies. Whatever you talk about, NEVER TALK ABOUT YOURSELF; ABOUT WHAT YOU

THINK, and certainly NEVER ABOUT YOUR DISAPPOINT-
MENTS and the STATE OF YOUR HEALTH, which generally
means the want of it in some particular. Let them
talk, and you be the listener—if you have the time.
When you do talk, let it be some subject you are
interested in, Music, Business, Improvements, or whatever else you truly feel and realise would be beneficial
to the community. It will be as well to leave religion
and politics alone. As to the first, see that you square
your own life. That is the main thing. Religion is
really a matter of living. To go out of our way to
attempt to force men to worship our own particular
idol is absurd. It is a waste of valuable time and an
impertinence.

In matters of religion let every man think for himself.
It is not what others think, but that which you yourself
believe, which makes or mars. Never despise a man
for the simple reason that he holds religious ideas
differing from your own. Give him credit for having
reasons for his convictions as you have for yours. The
man who has no convictions is the man whom you have
most need to fear—no moral standing of right and
wrong—but it is no part of your business to condemn or
ostracise him. It is for him to think these matters out
for himself, to live his own life, and take the consequence, even as you must yourself. If you have no
definite religious views, so much the worse for yourself.
There can be no Self-reliance, Personal Magnetism, and
Will-power, where one has no faith in one's own worth
and integrity—no sterling, binding convictions which

help him to possess either of these qualities. But no man of sense brawls with his neighbours and the world about creeds, traditions, plate washings, communion cups, vestments, or candles. Be fully persuaded in your own mind. Let it be a worthy persuasion and live up to it.

It is not what you say or profess to believe, but your life, which will be the truest testimony to your real thought and convictions. Truly "as a man thinketh in his heart so is he." Let your thoughts be frank, kindly, and manly—expressed or not—and your life itself will proclaim the true manhood. True religion is shown in sympathy and straight dealing to your fellow-men. Fellow-men meaning among the rest, our women folk, wife, children, dependents. There is only one religion for you—it is that which appeals best to the noblest features in your manhood, and which helps to make you a better man. That is the standard for you.

"Sensible men are all of the same religion" remarks Waldenshare in *Endymion*. "Pray what is that?" asked the Prince. "Sensible men never tell," replies Waldenshare. Although this is a Disraelian sarcasm, it is a shrewd maxim. This is not the place for a homily on religion, which is exemplified in the lives of noble and true souls. It is merely a suggestion. Whatever your religious convictions are, be true to them and let them manifest in reliability, manhood, character, or true worth.

Politics can be best expressed in the secrecy of the ballot box. Never be tempted to criticise your superiors in their absence. That will do you more harm than good. When in doubt, be nice, say nothing, whoever else may do the most of the talking. FOR THE MAN WHO RESERVES HIS OPINIONS, KNOWS WHEN TO KEEP SILENT, HAS ALREADY GOT HOLD OF THE KEY OF SUCCESS.

In speaking or in writing, however much inclined, never be in a hurry. Never say an unpleasant thing or a smart thing—although clever—which is likely to be misunderstood or which hurts the feelings. Never say in writing that which can some day be just as well spoken. That which can be borne and also be effective when spoken becomes very severe, harsh, and offensive when written. Keep this in your mind's eye, when either making reports or in writing to friends. Business letters should be brief and always courteous, whether accepting, declining, or making a request. And, as a matter of sound judgment, never send circulars or write when either can be substituted by a personal interview.

Reserve commands respect from superiors and obedience from inferiors. Friendship and Business should not be mixed; neither should we be on terms of intimacy with those whom, in the order of things, we are to control or command. Those with whom you come into contact, in the way of duty, business, or socially, may be coarse, refined, vulgar, sarcastic, abusive, or gifted with the gentle art of Blarney. Enjoy what you can in your own way. What you cannot, let it be to you like water on a duck's back. Whatever you do, ON NO ACCOUNT ALLOW YOURSELF TO

BE EITHER UPSET OR THROWN OFF YOUR GUARD by either ABUSE OR PRAISE.

BE STILL. NEVER MIND YOUR OWN FEELINGS. WAIT, LET THEM HAVE THEIR SAY, and so get at their MIND or their WANTS. Life is too short to waste time studying one's feelings. IN MANHOOD there is no room for that sort of thing. A MAN IS ABOVE IT. YOU ARE ABOVE IT. IF NOT, MAKE A POINT TO BE SO. Never —don't get tired of these nevers for a little yet— NEVER ENTER INTO A DISCUSSION EITHER TO DEFEND YOUR CHARACTER OR IN ORDER TO BE UNDERSTOOD, and certainly NEVER BECAUSE YOUR DIGNITY HAS BEEN OFFENDED. LIFE IS TOO SHORT FOR THIS. You may say as a rule—"The silent man is the strong man, and wins all along the line."

THERE IS NO DOUBT THAT THE CONTROL OF THE TONGUE MAKES FOR STRENGTH OF WILL IN THE INDIVIDUAL, AND ENHANCES HIS POWER TO INFLUENCE, DIRECT, AND CONTROL OTHERS.

In this lesson I am dealing with some of the most desirable attitudes of conduct to take up, rather than laying emphasis on some wonderful secret by the aid of which one is enabled to take advantage of one's fellows. These lessons are based on a close acquaintance with the Laws of Harmony, and the conclusion is, the straighter, the cleaner, and the squarer a man is and means to be in dealing with his fellows, THE GREATER WILL BE HIS POWER TO DEAL WITH THEM EFFECTUALLY.

I want you to come to the simple and direct conclusion that to be of any service in the world—your particular world;—to understand yourself; to be fit to occupy your right groove; to exercise a healthy influence over your fellows—ay, and to be benefited by them—and lastly, but by no means least, to prolong your days, you must live your healthiest, best, sanest, most moral, spiritual, and most reasonable life.

Soul, brain, and body—mind and body—are united in this life; whatever benefits the one helps the other. Whatever degrades, demoralises the one, reacts unfavourably on the other. I need not dwell on this. It is enough to call your attention to it, as a guide for present and future conduct. Let it be the KEYNOTE to all subsequent procedure. Let Temperance, Self-control, Moderation, and REASONABLE RESERVE, become your Stepping Stones to your SUCCESS IN LIFE.

It may be safely said that "the exercise of Man's Moral and Spiritual Nature—the higher and finer sentiments of Man—elevate, tone, purify, and add not only to bodily health, but to the Mental powers of the Man. Whereas, neglecting the exercise of the foregoing mental qualities—which distinguish the man from the lower animals—and living almost wholly in the exercise of his other powers—even intellectually, but without their elevating influence — pleasure, enjoyment, and even health of a kind may be possible. But in the end, the mere exercise and gratification of man's animal passions, instincts, appetites, prematurely undermines the constitutional forces, and makes for earlier breakdowns in the physical organisation, long before that stage could be possibly reached by living soundly and moderately in all departments of being, under the quickening stimulus of the higher qualities of the Mind and Thought-power."

In living your best life one is sure to live their happiest and longest life. Let your line of life be one of living your BEST LIFE TO-DAY. To-morrow may be yours; it is not yours. Whether yours or not, neither count on it, dread it, nor discount it. JUST LIVE TO-DAY your best, brightest, sweetest, and most wholesome life, and whatever lies in the future, you are laying such a foundation, that, come weal or woe—whatever it may be—you will be all the firmer, brighter, more self-controlled, and the better able to make the best use of that which is to come. You will do more than that; by acting on the foregoing hints, you will make that which is to come—come in the way which you will be best fitted and able to make the most of.

At the danger of making repetitions, in order to emphasise what has been advanced, permit me to say, we are constituted of Spirit, Soul, Mind, and Body, one great whole. No mere physical cleanliness will make up for impurity of Mind. And no religious ceremonies will make up for the neglect of the laws of physical health. No brilliancy of intellect will make up for what is called "Heart," or soul, kindly feeling and decency. To get the most good out of life, we must live our BEST, SWEETEST, TRUEST, and ALL-ROUND LIFE TO-DAY. Nothing else is required or can be better. Should to-morrow come, or should it never come to you in this life of Time and Space Conceptions, that life will be the best life to live—ONE THE MOST FRUITFUL OF GOOD TO OTHERS AND TO SELF.

You know that Man stands at the apex of organised life, and that he has power, which he does not, unhappily, exercise as he should, of living a healthy physical, a healthy mental, and a healthy moral life, ALL IN ONE. Animals do well, acting in obedience to Instinct. But man possesses less instinct than the animals, and he is endowed by higher qualities of intellect, moral and spiritual power, although he may and does not make the best use of these. He can guide himself into health of body and power of mind, IF HE SO DECIDES. HE CAN DIRECT, HOLD, AND CONTROL THOUGHT equally as well as decide such minor actions as to eat, not to eat; walk, or not to walk; restrain himself or not, as the case may be, in the ordinary walks of life. What is it that you want to give up? What is it that you want to do? Are you realising that there are some defects in character that you will be better without and that there are some qualities which you want to strengthen? Good. I am glad to hear that. You can accomplish WHATEVER YOUR HEART IS SET UPON, and HEALTH, HAPPINESS, AND POWER AND USEFULNESS ARE YOURS, IF YOU WILL HAVE IT SO. WORK AS WELL AS PRAY.

WORK IS THE REALISATION OF THOUGHT IN PRACTICE, whether it be Sculpture, Painting, Music, polishing a boot, or one's conduct.

PRAYER is Aspiration. Work is the life outcome

of that aspiration. In a word, THINK RIGHT and YOU WILL LIVE RIGHT.

"Silence is the element in which great things fashion themselves together," says Carlyle, "that, at length, they may emerge, full-formed and majestic, into the daylight of life, which they are henceforth to rule." Treasure Silence for thinking, planning, cultivating your own powers, and, above all, treasure it as a means of Self-control and a step towards Masterfulness.

Think over the foregoing lesson, and then commence. Don't take yourself too seriously. To be a good man, you need not be either a prig or a pedant. Just be a decent, kindly, patient, good-natured, cheerful person, and, above all, capable of "kenning yer ain ken, an' mindin' yer ain business."

CHAPTER VI

HOW TO CULTIVATE WILL-POWER

"Everything yields before the strong and earnest will. It grows by exercise. It excites confidence in others, while it takes to itself the lead. Difficulties before which mere cleverness fails, and which leave the irresolute prostrate and helpless, vanish before it. They only do not impede its progress, but it often makes them stepping stones to a higher and more enduring triumph."—DR TULLOCH.

IN this lesson we take another step forward. It is by *one step at a time that the roughest road is covered or the most difficult hill ascended.* A step is a little thing in itself, but a great thing according to the *Spirit*, perseverance, and the direction in which each step is taken. A drop of water is a little thing, but drop after drop will wear the hardest stone, provided each drop falls on the same place. The tap of a hammer is not much, but repeated and applied in the same direction —not first one way and then another—on the head of a nail, it will be driven truly and effectively home. These are truisms which everybody knows, and which nearly everybody forgets to apply mentally. The man who lacks Concentration, and allows his thoughts to run hither and thither, forgets them. Instead of pulling in his thoughts and ranging them in something like order and marshalling them in a *given direction*—although he talks big, and possibly thinks a lot of honour and success and what he would do—lets them run away with him—to Failure. Step by step; drop on drop ; blow on blow ; *thought following thought*, in *a given direction*, not only MEANS SUCCESS, but OBTAINS IT.

In this lesson we will enter into more practical details, which, if observed and *practised*, will assuredly make for Success, Health, and Happiness in life. In the former lessons I have given you hints and general advice, meant to form Motive Keys for immediate and future action. These Keys will recommend themselves to whatever is best in you ; that which your judgment esteems good and useful, that seize and follow up. Do not practise ardently for a week or a month, and then lose interest. That is not the way to win battles over the enemy or—what is more important—gain victories over yourself. You may say:

"I fully approve of all you say, and I can fully appreciate all the benefits which are sure to arise from the course you suggest, but I should like to have some simple directions of a more personal character, by which I can improve myself, increase my WILL-POWER, industrial and business aptitudes, effectiveness in social intercourse, and naturally my influence over and with others. Can these be obtained, and how ?"

All these can be obtained. The "how ?" as may be surmised, is a matter of self-discipline, and the determination to carry out the instructions in a quiet, thorough, and intelligent way into all the departments

of life—public and *private*. I emphasise *private*, for
this simple reason, if you allow yourself to get into
slipshod ways and levity of thought and action in
private, it will not be a matter of surprise if these
weaknesses find expression in public. THEY ALWAYS
DO. What we are in heart, in private, is revealed
sooner or later in our public life. Private life is the
foundation of all public Successes and Failures.

The Moral Courage which characterises the public
career of the men and women we most esteem, or
should esteem; the Courage to seek the truth and be
TRUE; the Courage to be patient, kind, as well as just;
to have Courage to be silent under great provocation;
to be honest under great temptations of popularity,
personal advancement, and the acquirement of wealth;
and the Courage to do one's duty, in whatever walk of
life, is a Courage which does not come with the blare
of trumpets or by the inspiring marshalling sound of
music, or even of the helpful example of some of our
fellows, but by developing that Courage from honest
convictions, and practising the same in private.

It is quite true that most men—and women too—
are more guarded or on their best behaviour in public
than in private; but notwithstanding all that care, the
influences and *habits* of good or ill, of thought or the
want of it, which dominate the private life, will, in
spite of all care to conceal them, break out and exhibit
themselves in public life.

The acquirement of a strong Will, of right habits
and a steady and earnest purpose in private life, will

not make life less sweet, amiable, or genial in public.
Far from doing so, self-discipline will enhance whatever is good ; and as to what is or may be termed evil,
it will render you either better able to STAND THE
FRICTIONS ARISING THEREFROM, or, better still, enable
you to OVERCOME, DOMINATE, and be MASTER. You will
not be the creature of circumstances, or blown about
by every whim, fancy, and desire of unregulated
passions, fears, and emotions, but the controller of your
circumstances and the MASTER of YOURSELF—A MAN.
Whatever you decide to do, you will do it. If you
labour for SUCCESS, it is yours.

Before we pass on, it will be well to pause, and
consider what is habit. To allow thoughts to run in
certain grooves, produces desires ; and desires dwelt upon
soon find expression in action. Actions repeated form
" Habits," and these habits—*unless under the dominance
of the judgment*—become largely automatic—self-acting
and self-gratifying—and control the man, instead of the
man controlling, directing, or, if need be, suppressing
the habit. No need to mention any particular habit.
But those which minister to the propensities, which are
exercised for their mere gratification, regardless of the
right or the wrong of it, are the worst possible to
acquire or possess. There are habits of omission which
are desirable to get rid of too, and of these the worst I
think is—what think you ?—Procrastination. Whatever you desire most to accomplish, COMMENCE NOW.

It would be too long, as well as too technical a
subject, to deal with Mind and the mental machinery

of the brain and the nerves; but it will be to the point
to mention, as illustrative of mental action, that
thoughts repeated—whether of their own sweet will, or
guided—cut a groove, as it were, in the brain substance
and corresponding and associated nerve connections
throughout the organisation, and the more frequently
repeated the deeper the channels, and the easier the
flow and the more powerful the habit. Take what is
called "Impulse" as an illustration. You find that
many men who pride themselves on intellect, soundness
of judgment—and many who don't—have their weak
point of character, and strongest flaw, in "Impulse."
This is shown in the unguarded tendency to speak;
to express annoyance; to criticise; to lose temper; to
express fear; to lust, covet, or to manifest certain
traits—good or ill—*impulsively.* These habits of
thought which have been allowed to dominate them
are often said to be hereditary, but are in the main
acquired. The man of weak convictions is content to
drift, and let himself go on the flowing tide of his
emotions and take pleasure out of them, recognising
them not as defects, and excusing his actions as being
"natural" or "just human nature." While he in
whom an awareness of defects is aroused, seeks to
master and restrict his emotions—impulses—and bring
all under the guidance of his awakened judgment and
more cultured intellect, and the moral forces of his
disciplined WILL.

Whatever is undesirable must be conquered by the
acquirement of better habits, and the old grooves, from

want of practice, will become filled up—so to speak—
while the new and better habits will have cut appropriate trenches for themselves. A little restraint,
always repeated, and repeated whenever the impulse
arises, will in time effectually check it. Whatever the
impulse is, check it. If you will do this, and continue
to do it, then you will become Master of yourself; for
whatever is inimical to your well-being is to be controlled, and thus whatever is best, worthy, and noble,
is not only allowed freer and fuller expression, but in
time becomes a part of self, by deliberate intention and
determination on your part. *Impulse*—undisciplined
emotions—expressed on the lines of the least resistance
and self-gratification, no longer control you, or the
Man, but the Man controls the *Impulse*.

I trust that this theme is sufficiently clear, and is
one which you can readily illustrate either from your
own experience or that of others. However, it is best
to see your own defects and rectify these—those of
friends and the world can be best left to rectify themselves. The man who loses (?) his temper may have
many admirable qualities, but he is not a Success,
for the simple reason that he lacks self-control and
is unreliable and given to extremes, and always more
or less dangerous and erratic. You know the man ; you
have often met him. " He's a very fine fellow, clever,
you know, but——" Having said so much, a few
words now on Self-control will be found of service.

We are able to manage others best in proportion as we are able to control ourselves.

One of the simplest and most effective methods of Self-control—having many beneficial reactions in health, character, WILL-POWER, and in Concentration—*is the habit of keeping the mouth shut and breathing through the nose.* If this is not natural to you, commence just now and make it natural.

"KEEP THE MOUTH SHUT AND BREATHE THROUGH THE NOSE."

There is nothing very occult or mysterious about this direction. In fact, it is very prosaic and common-place. But if you want to ward off disease, increase your vital and virile energies, increase the purity of your blood, stimulate as well as perfect the heart's action, and supply the brain and the sensory, motor, and vegetative or sympathetic nervous systems with the material necessary to do their work, KEEP the mouth SHUT and breathe through the NOSE.

BY AN EFFORT OF THE WILL—in the one direction—EXERCISED IN PRIVATE AND IN PUBLIC, KEEP THE MOUTH SHUT AND BREATHE THROUGH THE NOSE.

The nose was made by the Great Architect of our being to breathe through, and the breathing in this way conduces to health, self-control, and well-being. Old men and women have instinctively gone through life with their mouths shut, and breathe through their nostrils, this being one of the foremost factors in their long life. Apart from the fact that the outward air is tempered and purified thereby before it passes into the lungs, a greater or fuller quantity of air is taken into the lungs; the chest is expanded and the whole system is benefited by the operation ; and last, though not least, the WILL TO DO AND TO DARE and the GRIT TO ACCOMPLISH THINGS IS PERFECTED THEREBY.

All animals breathe through the nostrils, and—except from wounds, accidents, and where they are unnaturally brought up, through the influence of and contact with man—run their allotted course, and in no case die prematurely. Of the savage and semi-civilised races, who, like the Indians of North and South America, breathe through the nose, where they are not devital-ised by the vices, drinks, and habits of the civilised (?) white man, the same may be said — longevity is characteristic. Notwithstanding their comparative lack of comfort and the many advantages which we enjoy, infant mortality is practically unknown among them, and old age a prevailing characteristic. The bravery, fortitude, valour, determination, and firmness, with physical endurance, of the Indian in his *native state*, are matters on which all great travellers are agreed. Unhappily, infantile mortality, premature decay, and a host of preventable diseases, with, alas ! too high a death rate, appears to be the lot of the open-mouthed white man. It would take too long to enter into this matter. Suffice it to say, you will notice that all really strong and able men—men of force, firmness, strength of Will, and dominating their fellows, and who have, within historic times, and within your own ex-perience, made their mark in science, politics, religion, the army of commerce, have been and are—physically and mentally too—men who have KEPT THE MOUTH SHUT.

Keep your mouth shut, and only open it when you want to clean your teeth, partake of food, or to speak, and then only when you have thought over—and the motive—what you are to say. No more impulsive spurts, no words of anger or impatience, and wounded self-conceit, if you would be a strong man, and a good man, in the best sense of these words.

You will notice, that while the open-mouthed may have many good qualities, they have no tenacity and staying power. The blow-hard and the blusterer sometimes talk with those who do not know better, but you may take it for certain that the man who is always talking about himself, and sometimes to himself, of his cleverness, and the misdeeds of friends or the world— poor old World!—the wrongdoings in politics and religion, and especially of what he "intends to do, or what he is not going to do," to say nothing about the man with the "Time-enough-to-morrow-motto"—never succeeds. The lack of success is due to want of one of the first essentials of Self-control, *reserve*—the silent tongue—physiognomically indicated by the shut mouth.

The habit of keeping the mouth shut in the day-time has many advantages, and in time, by a process of education, that habit will be carried out in sleep, with still greater advantage to health. There will be no snoring caused by unnatural breathing—forced air-draughts through the mouth—no nightmares, arrested breathing and sudden deaths in consequence—frequently attributed to heart failure—when the breathing is correctly performed through the nose during sleep. There is *no tired feeling* in the morning. *Sleeping with the shut mouth is truly restorative.*

Now, if the vital powers are improved; health maintained and conserved; disease resisted ; life made more enjoyable and *prolonged*, by the simple expedient of keeping the *mouth shut*, it is well worth the trial. If you add to this that the practice conduces to Firmness, Decision, Perseverance, Fortitude, Concentration, and Strength of Will, the *exercise* becomes a delightful and pleasant necessity. When I add to this that the practice is in harmony with the evident requirements of our nature—the nostrils as air passages, the mouth for food, etc.—the wise man, that is you, who wishes to acquire sound and good habits of life and Self-control, to say nothing of a useful habit in conformity with the structure and function of breathing, will at once commence the practice ; then by perseverance and constant watchfulness will keep it up, until it becomes *second nature*—automatic—and is thereafter carried out without the conscious supervision of the ordinary, every-day mind. The aim should be to form a new and correct habit of breathing with intention, and the exercise being under intellectual supervision and controlled by intentional volition—apart from the manifold benefits to health, all very important—the practice in itself will conduce to *strength of* WILL, the development of the WILL being one of the main objects of taking these lessons.

When you see two men stripped for a fight—and

some men will fight,—and you see one with an open mouth, and the other with firmly shut mouth, "you will put your money on the wrong horse," to use a vulgarism, if you expect the former will come off best in the tussle.

It will not be out of place to mention that it is especially dangerous for persons of weak lungs to breathe through the mouth, and it is courting disease for healthy persons to do so, thus inhaling, without the slightest protection, dust, filth, animalised exhalations and diseased germs held in suspension in the air, whether in the dusty road or the crowded hall, not to mention the improperly ventilated living and bed-rooms. All breathing should be done through the nose. Where the air is imperfect, you minimise the dangers, while obtaining the full advantage of whatever is good by breathing thus correctly. By breathing through the nose, the air circulates in and through the Eustachian tubes, by which the oxygen is collected, the system built up, certain matters consumed or converted into heat, the blood purified, and the brain and nerves restored and refreshed. Whether walking, running, hill-climbing, thinking, waking or sleeping, the fullest benefits are to be obtained by this, the only CORRECT MODE OF BREATHING.

It may take a little time to overcome the old and learn the new and better way. The new habit will soon make in the brain substance a groove or grooves or fresh lines of nerve tracks for itself to travel on, and become as much a matter of course as the old impulses, which you mean and are working to get rid of.

Persistent effort should overcome the old and pernicious habit in the course of three or four weeks. WHERE THERE IS A WILL THERE IS A WAY. And in this case, the WAY is to make up your mind and COMMENCE AT ONCE. Presently you will know something more about SUGGESTION and AUTO-SUGGESTION, and you will be able to still further increase your WILL-POWER, and overcome this or any other bad habit or weakness. Just all you have to do is SHUT your MOUTH and BREATHE THROUGH YOUR NOSE, and when you manage this, you will be able to say " I WILL, and I CAN," to some purpose. The region of philosophic doubt, with its lack of vitality and actions, will be passed; you will cross the Jordan, and enter the region of the " I AM, and I DO," in the practical realisation of Self-poised Manhood.

Most people do not think about breathing, unless there is some difficulty in the way, and for the foregoing reason they seldom *breathe* DEEPLY ENOUGH, and consequently have not the Health, the VIM, *or live long enough.* One cannot always take cognisance of one's breathing, but it will be well at stated times daily, morning, afternoon, and night, either in bedroom, before an open window, or when out in the " open," to *practise deliberately and very firmly,* and there with INTENTION, DEEP BREATHING, something after this fashion :—

Close the mouth, and then slowly, steadily, and firmly

inhale through the nostrils while counting five slowly; retain the breath, while counting five; and then, by a special effort of the Will, exhale as slowly and as smoothly as you can. Pause again for five seconds or so, and then repeat the process for at least twenty times, at one trial. The following times will be found most convenient—before rising, when the exercise may be carried out lying on your back, all the body muscles flexed, except those brought into play by the breathing; in the afternoon, from five to ten minutes in some quiet spot, either in your rooms, or outside: lying or standing, carry out the exercise as best you can; at night, just after retiring, and before going to sleep. Leave off thinking; let everything else go; go in for this exercise. Practise breathing, in an even, soft, slow, and quiet way, and then drop asleep, and aim at having SOUND SLEEP IN YOUR MIND.

Continue this form of Deep Breathing, with Intention, for at least a fortnight, and then take up the next exercise which will be given, and you will soon reap the benefits of the exercise in Mind and body. All that has been advanced is on the lines of Health, Self-control, and Will-power.

CHAPTER VII

HOW TO CULTIVATE WILL-POWER—*continued*

"Have a purpose in life . . . and having it, throw such strength of mind and muscle into thy work as has been given thee."—CARLYLE.

"IN the course of a day an adult breathes about twenty-six hundred gallons of air, weighing thirty-four pounds, which is about six times the average amount of food and drink consumed. The conclusion is that we should one and all be just six times as careful that the air we breathe is as pure as that our food and drink is unadulterated. But are we?" asked an athlete, in one of the local papers recently. On this matter I will say a few words.

"To breathe is to live" is a true statement of an essential fact, and also a text well worthy of the highest exposition. Space will only admit of a few suggestions. It can be said that incorrect breathing lies at the physical foundation of incorrect living, and in that way the majority live but half their days because they do not breathe deeply enough, and as they breathe mostly through their mouths, they literally court disease—in ignorance. Situated as many are at home and abroad, the atmosphere is not what it should be; but despite this fact, they swallow the air by the throat, with all its vile admixtures of dust particles, animal exhalations, micro-organisms, carbonic gas, and the more or less putrescent matter formed by our tissues and thrown off, with other devitalising stuff, etc., without the protection, and the air filtering, which the nostrils are designed by Nature to give. That is bad enough, but it is not all.

Many do not breathe deeply enough. As the result there remains in the lungs a much larger amount of *residual air*, partially stagnant, from want of renewal, and becomes in itself foul, poisonous, and an ever-present source of disease.

To breathe correctly, that should be done through the nostrils. And at definite times, fuller, more thorough, and deeper breathing should be practised, with intention, and whatever is best in the air will be taken to sustain a healthy life, and the unsuitable will be rejected.

By correct breathing, whatever is best in the atmosphere is taken into the lungs, and whatever is unsuitable is rejected, with the result, greater PITH, Vim, and driving power is given to the whole mental and physical forces of the individual, and Personal Magnetism, which is the sum-total of these forces, is developed.

Whatever are the constituent properties of the air—Ozone, Argon, Oxygen, Nitrogen—aqueous vapour—and ammonia,—the main end of breathing is to obtain an adequate supply of the vital sustaining gas in the atmosphere—oxygen—which is essential to the life work of every nerve cell, substance, and tissue in the organisation.

All changes which take place in the organisation,
whether by thought, emotion, or movement, conscious
or otherwise, are always accompanied with the development of carbonic acid gas. This is highly poisonous
and must be removed. Breathing then consists of
the *inhalation of Oxygen and the expiration of Carbonic
Acid Gas; the breathing in of vitality, health, power,
and the casting off of debris in the form of poisonous
and disease-burdened gases.* Breathing thus, under the
control of the WILL, that is with intention, is a
most beneficial, rejuvenating, recuperating operation
physically, and gives power and tone to the mind in
a remarkable degree. Put the directions into practice
for a few short months, and you will not only breathe
more fully, deeply, and correctly, instinctively, but you
will become practically a re-made, younger, newer,
fresher, better, brighter, and a stronger man.

Perhaps you say that your life is too busy; your
work is too hard; that it comes in fits and starts; that
you have no time, and all that. You will find that
nothing is too hard to do, where you are interested;
that you have had a lot of time and perhaps spent it
worse. There is always time for dreaming, shirking,
and drifting; time for folly, disease, and death, some
of which time might be spared to fit oneself for a
healthier life—a life of health and purpose. *Make it
your business to find the time and reap the benefits.*

Ordinary breathing is carried on under the direction
of a special automatism, and hence is not—in the
majority of cases — influenced or directed by the

individual. Inspiration and expiration take about four seconds, or fifteen times to the minute, or about once to four beats of the heart. In physical exercise, the depth, the length, and the volume will be increased while the breathing periods will become less in number. In disease, it is the other way about : the volume of air taken into the lungs is less, and the breathing periods shorter and much more frequent, rising to fifty or sixty times a minute. I might add, the more frequent the periods the greater the nerve expansion and exhaustion.

It is well to notice that, in ordinary conditions, in our unconscious breathing the lungs expand and contract once to four beats of the heart. In more vigorous and active physical exercise, once to six, seven, or more beats; in low and exhausting conditions, the periods correspond to one or two beats of the heart. Without going into details, adequate—that is full, deep, and continuous breathing—is necessary to well-being. Not only is there carbonic air to get rid of by each expiration, but the breathing must be deeper and fuller at times, to change the character of the residual air to purer and healthier conditions.

Suppose we say that the maximum capacity of the lungs is 330 cubic inches. Deduct from this 100 cubic inches for residual air—a volume never less than this always remains in the lungs during life. With this deduction, there is left a capacity for 230 cubic inches of air. This is called the *vital* capacity, as distinct from the *maximum* or total capacity of the lungs. There is seldom less than 230 cubic inches in the lungs during

an ordinary inspiration. By ordinary breathing—
that which takes place automatically—we take in and
give out about 30 cubic inches of air. This is called
the *Tidal* air. This tidal air is ever flowing in and out
without the conscious supervision of the mind. It is
enough to live and to vegetate, but not enough for
work, energy, and to suit the end of a purposeful life.
The lungs are expanded, although not dilated. By
deep breathing we can take in another 100 cubic inches
of air, and this is called *Complemental* air. The sum of
the air capacity of the lungs consists of the residual, the
vital capacity, the tidal, and the complementary air.
We breathe as we grow without thinking about it, but
it will serve our purpose to notice that in ordinary
breathing, the tidal flow only amounts to 30 or so cubic
inches, and that by exercise or effort—still unconsciously—we increase the quantity; but in Deep
Breathing under the direction and the Control of the
WILL, the lungs are dilated to their fullest maximum
capacity, and this can be done with a little regular
practice, without straining and in a very simple and
natural way. We complement the tidal breathing by
100 or so cubic inches of air, and consequently are not
only benefited by the greater consumption of fresh air,
but are benefited by the throwing off from the lungs
of a greater quantity of carbonic gas—the products of
internal breathing.

During one's waking hours, the breathing is a little
fuller than during sleep. We may take 4 or 5 cubic
inches more air in tidal breathing when awake, but

this I maintain is not sufficient. This is shown by the fact that when any exertion is made, called forth by labour, or even by thought, the respirations deepen. Here is Nature's object lesson, that for an active, energetic, industrious life, in which a clear head, good physical health and self-control are essential, full and deep breathing is an absolute necessity. It therefore follows, if we wish to fit ourselves for an industrious, useful, healthy, and happy life, the practice of, and the deliberate control of deeper, fuller, and at the same time correct breathing is a valuable preparation.

I urge you to learn early and master the art of breathing properly. CLOSE THE MOUTH AND BREATHE THROUGH THE NOSE, AT ALL TIMES—DAY AND NIGHT. IF YOU LEARN TO DO SO DURING the DAY—by systematic and regular practice—you will in time breathe properly at NIGHT. It is possible while speaking, and even, sometimes, when eating—all mastication should be done with a closed mouth—to breathe through the nostrils, and although one may breathe when speaking through the mouth, even this can be reduced to a minimum. The daily practice of breathing through the nose will soon be carried out during the sleeping hours, with the refreshing result of having a better night's sleep, and therefore greater fitness and self-control to battle with life's work and problems during the day.

In addition to breathing with the mouth shut, learn to breathe deeply, at stated times each day, for the reasons already given, and in due time what has been a conscious and careful performance will pass into the

region of the automatic—the mouth will be kept shut
and the breathing will be deeper, and your physical
and mental powers will be enhanced.   Greater Personal
Magnetism, Attractiveness, Self-control, Will-power, and
Concentration will be yours.   Think of the advantage
these will be in any walk in life, public and private.
Think of the greater ease and less friction with which
you will be able to approach and attack your work ;
think of your increased influence for good with your
fellows ; think of the benefits to your physical and
mental health ; all this and more having its foundation
in the conscious perfection in the practice of breathing.
The practice costs nothing, and the reward is great.
Have the pluck and give these directions a fair and
square trial, and for three months, three times each day,
for at least five minutes—ten if possible—practise deep
breathing.   Let your periods run to ten or fifteen
seconds, not more, and you will prove to yourself what
great good can be achieved by a little persistent effort.
COMMENCE TO-DAY.   PRACTISE IN SECRET.

A great deal of mysterious rubbish—pretentious
talk—has been written about various modes of Occult
breathing for the attainment of this power and that.
To our Western practical mind, it is good enough to
breathe *as the lark breathes*—the lion, and as any
healthy, vigorous man should breathe—*in a full-chested
natural manner*.   Our healthy ancestors breathed thus,
but the dwellers in cities, pursuing their sedentary and
artificially stimulated lives, have forgotten the way.
Any exercises suggested in this course are an attempt

to bring back, under the control and impulse of healthier, happier thoughts, good, honest, deep, full-chested breathing.

To mention one tithe of the blessings which flow in the train of correct breathing would require a separate work on the subject, but we can notice in passing a few :—

First, although not the most important, is that exhilaration of feeling and general alertness of mind and body which come from the expanded lungs; the purification of the blood; the actual magnetisation of its corpuscles, through the more perfect oxidation which takes place; the more perfect action of the heart; a fuller and better supply of aliment for brain and nerve matter, as organs for the manifestation of Mind.

Secondly, a fitness to DO and DARE; grit and back-bone, in the place of backwardness, flabbiness, sensitiveness, and fear to see and to seize the right time and the way to accomplish what should be done, by ourselves.

Thirdly, our greater power to influence others, through our increased strength of character, self-control, reserve, as well as words, fitly spoken, by which we discharge our duties, and get others to do theirs. Men who spend hours sucking a pipe, and fiddling with cigarettes, do not know of the joy and vigour which full and deep breathing gives one.

A writer in the *Young Man* on the Secret of Long Life, after making several recommendations, extols the benefit of deep breathing thus :—

There is another valuable habit as a health and

longevity practice, to which I would like to draw the attention of those of the readers of the *Young Man* who are unacquainted with it—namely, the definite, deliberate, and daily practice of deep breathing; nasal breathing, abdominal breathing. This is really a very vitalising exercise. It contributes to a much more complete oxygenation of the blood, and a saturation of the whole system with the life-giving fluid, than does ordinary breathing. It has a potent mental influence as well. As briefly hinted above, the restless life of our time conduces to excitement, agitation, irritability, and shallow, semi-chest breathing, and thus to devital-isation. Deep breathing has a remarkably controlling influence on the emotions; it counteracts and controls these, and calms the whole being, so that it has a dual influence on health and life—from the mental as well as the physical side. It is thus also an aid to quiet reflection and meditation. And all the while you are breathing and meditating let the *mind* be kept in a receptive, responsive attitude, open—so to speak—to Divine impressions, influences, impulses and intuitions, which—*mark you*—OBEY. But the reader is mentally inquiring concerning the *modus operandi*. Here it is: Either lie flat on your back and put your hands behind the head, or stand or sit erect with shoulders well back. Simply *slowly* inhale through the nostrils until both chest and stomach are fairly fully expanded ; then *as slowly* exhale until both are fully evacuated. Repeat this from six to twelve times, twice daily, or as occasion may require.

By correct breathing we increase the internal energy—that is, the circulation of the blood and the action of the lungs, the functioning of the heart and other organs—and thus the internal respiration is perfected. The internal respiration occurs in the deepest parts of the organisation. We never think, move, but with every thought and action we take a certain amount of Oxygen out of the blood, and supply in exchange a quantity of carbonic gas from the tissues which passes into the blood vessels. The renewed blood speeds away on its mission of healing and mercy and returns laden with effete matter and gases, which the system must get rid of before it can carry on its normal work in a healthy or frictionless manner.

While a temperate and healthily active and in-dustrious life helps, more or less, to furnish the conditions of well-being pointed out—*greater power is obtained by consciously and deliberately practising Breathing, Deep Breathing, with intent and concentration.* None can have magnetic and healing power whose blood is anæmic; neither can they have a thorough influence over others, if they cannot control their impulses—the Breath.

Personal Magnetism is a real thing, and in these latter days has been abundantly demonstrated, by means of delicate instruments, and by psychometrical experimentation, in the existence of "N" rays, and by other methods; also in the power to cure disease, possessed by some persons, and not by others. This Magnetism flows out from all, as emanations from a piece of Radium. Restless, excitable people waste it. All neurotics, or neurasthenic, as well as sensual and hysterical persons, waste their vital powers, Magnetism, faster than they can accumulate or generate it. Restlessness and excitability, which shows itself in strong emotions and selfish anxiety; in sharp, jerky motions; in tramping up and down, and placing the feet heavily on the ground ; in rocking in chairs ; in other needless movements keeping the body in incessant strain, and useless waste of nerve force ; bolting food ; excess in eating and drinking; gratifying the animal propensities injudiciously; and even in much lesser things, as twitching the limbs, drumming with the feet, biting nails, tapping with the fingers, parading and humming and whistling, and a host of other monotonous movements, which are kept up and are wasting vital energy and inducing bad habits, or needless exertion—none of them of real service to either the individual or anyone else—all these habits are to be avoided. If acquired, they must be got rid of.

AVOID WASTE. CULTIVATE the Art of Restfulness. In addition to the Breathing Exercises, it is a good thing to cultivate the habit of occasionally being very still, restful, and fixing the mind on one thought or idea, having in itself the germ of a worthy motive, be it Health, LOVE, SUCCESS. What you get thoroughly interested in, that you will do best. I will touch on this again, when I deal with Suggestion and its power.

Be as much in the fresh air as your circumstances

will allow. Breathe deeply at stated periods, daily. Take frequent baths; all from twenty to fifty years of age may with advantage take a sponge bath daily. Neatness and cleanliness without fuss are aids to the possession of a healthy influence. Don't be afraid of sunshine; give it body, heart, and house room. While it warms you externally, let the sunshine of your affections and cheerful disposition warm up your vital forces and irradiate healthy and attractive magnetism from you; so that your countenance and every act and pose will suggest Self-control, Self-reliance, and strength of purpose.

See that you have a good night's rest. Don't rob yourself of Sleep, by idle thinking or worrying. When you retire to rest, Rest and Sleep. There will be not only plenty of time for thought and action when you awake, but you will be able to do these things better for the rest and the sleep. If the night's rest be not enough to quieten and strengthen the nerves, find time to take an extra period during the day, say from half an hour to an hour, for perfect rest and privacy, and see that you get it. If you cannot get half an hour, be thankful for ten or fifteen minutes, and rest—lie still and shut your eyes; breathe peacefully and calmly and rest. And as you lie still, making no movements with hands, feet, fingers, or toes, and resist the temptation to move, you will find a sensation of nerve warmth and power creeping over you, something of comfort and possibly an inclination to sleep. Sleep, if you can spare the time; *rest anyway, a full rest, without move-*

ment and as little thinking as possible. Remember that the world can get on without you, but you cannot get on without rest. The more strenuous your duties and active daily life, the more you need rest, and systematic nerve rest.

If you are inclined to sleeplessness, you might adopt this nerve-rest plan at night. Close the eyes, and lie still; no twisting, turning, and twitching. When asleep, your body will do all the turning necessary for comfort. Your business is to go asleep. And when you awaken in the morning, after practising the Breathing Exercises, better get up. It is not a good plan to court the blankets, and drift into a second sleep approaching to *réveillé*. Better be up and doing. Make yourself spruce, and get to work, on whatever most needs your attention that day. "Every day a line," and so make headway.

In this lesson several matters have been touched upon: all easy exercises in the art of self-control. Keep them well in view. Practise daily. KEEP THE MOUTH SHUT. BREATHE THROUGH THE NOSTRILS. AT TIMES BREATHE DEEPLY, and PRACTISE the BREATHING EXERCISES. Attend to the other little hints. Do not waste energy doing useless things. Take rest when necessary. This does not mean to be idle or lazy. It means when you have work to do—*do it*; and when rest is required—*take it*. Never cheat yourself out of sleep, nor lie when you should be up.

CHAPTER VIII

THE WILL AND ITS DEVELOPMENT

"The question is not whether a man be a free agent—that is to say, whether he can write or forbear, speak or be silent, according to his will—but whether the will to write and the will to forbear come upon him according to his will, or according to anything else in his own power. I acknowledge this liberty, that I can do if I will; but to say I can will if I will, I take to be an absurd speech."—THOMAS HOBBES.

IN the last two lessons I have pointed out the value and the necessity of correct breathing, and have given a hint or two how fuller, deeper, and more energising breathing can be carried out. I will presume that at a little trouble and with some sensible determination— repeated and repeated efforts on your part—you have practised the exercises given in the previous lessons, and that you now find them comparatively easy of accomplishment. Anyway, keep up the practice for many months to come. Hygienically and mentally there is no more simple, valuable, or important exercise. Simple as it looks, both intelligent watchfulness and an *effort* of the Will are required to carry it into practice. Do not forget or postpone. That is not the way to acquire new and useful habits, or the way to get out of the old, irregular, anxious, and worrying way of thinking and doing things. Give the exercises full and fair play, and you will be astonished to find that you have been developing calmness of spirit and self-control all the time.

Do not excuse yourself on the ground that you have not time. Make the time. Do not excuse yourself because you find yourself forgetting—as if that was any real excuse for negligence. No man forgets that which he has a real interest in. If the Will is to be educated on new lines, there must be no negligence, and the correct mode of breathing must be formed and maintained. The Breathing Exercises are the first step, and from this it will be comparatively easy to take further steps on the road of Self-improvement and gain a greater degree of Magnetic Control and Personal Influence.

Before you can concentrate your thoughts in a certain definite line for half an hour, it will be well to attempt to do so for five minutes ; for four, for three, or even for one minute. Learn to do the latter and you will be able soon to do the former. Concentration in a given direction is essential to success. Before you can exercise your Will in great things, it is well to attempt to do so in ways that are esteemed small. In attempting to control others—whether directly or indirectly, matters little—you will succeed best in proportion to your command of self-control. Hence these hints in self-discipline. You cultivate self-discipline with a purpose. You see the folly of rushing through life anyhow ; obeying the beck of this impulse or that passion. You do not obey ; you control. You realise the stupidity of blundering through anyhow, of changing your mind, being fickle. You approach matters more calmly. Whatever the difficulty, you take time to fill your chest, and consider. You are determined to succeed, and what you take in hand, you do with definite aim and succeed. You are a man of decision, because you have learned to be decisive. You are a man of your word; you don't say much, because you mean what you say, and mean to keep true to your saying. To be strong and purposeful is your aim. You may not have reached the mark yet, but it is the goal at which you are aiming.

You can appreciate the self-reliant, energetic man ; one whom you can respect, obey, or be led by, should either be necessary. You prefer to consult one of that character or to have such an one represent you in the affairs of your district or county. The man who *does* things because he has the intelligence to do what is necessary, and who has the determination not to be baulked by trifles, or who is not held back by neurotic fears, is one whom you can approve. Such a man achieves Success, because he *knows* his own mind, and works for that Success ; he therefore guides, directs, organises, and influences others because he knows what he wants. What you really admire you can become. You can have strength and purposefulness. When you talk, let it be to the point, with an object clearly in view, although not necessarily expressed. All those who are under you only need to know what is required of them. Keep your own counsel. What they are told to do is sufficient for them. Work well done deserves a word of praise. Give that; it is encouragement. Do not muzzle the ox which treads out the corn. A word of appreciation always helps—some. Do not seek praise for yourself. Whether you meet with adulation or praise, opposition or contempt; whatever these may be, let them be incentives for the thorough prosecution of whatever is taken in hand. Do not let praise unduly elate or censure unduly depress. You pursue the course you have decided on, because of its inherent worth, regardless of either the praise or the blame. You will be the man to succeed, because you are disciplining your will; have calmly considered your difficulties; discounted the future, and aim to be and are sincere, steadfast, and reliable; and as such you may expect to do well, and better shape the management of your affairs in the near future.

I have spoken of Will so often, I think it is well that you should have some intelligent outline of what is Will. Like many other combined mental functions, it cannot be readily defined. Will is recognised as the power of choosing; mental power, by which we determine to do or refrain from doing something which we conceive to be within our power; the natural attribute of a moral and responsible agent; volition, determination, choice, one's power to determine or decide; command, direction, resolution, disposition, inclination, desire, etc.—these are various modes of expressing man's possession of that which is called Will. Good Will is an amicable expression of one's benevolent powers; Ill Will, of the evil or the reverse of the good; Strong Will, one's ability to carry wishes into practice ; Weak Will, indicating flabbiness of purpose, irresolution, indecision, etc.

Without any definition, you will, as most persons do, know what you mean by Will. You can feel it better than analyse it. It will be helpful to consider the matter for a little. *Will is a mode of motion of the Intellectual Faculties.* Although called a faculty by metaphysicians and psychologists, it is really the combined action of several faculties. Will is their executive function. In this connection, what is called a " Strong Mind," or a " Strong Will," a " Weak Mind," or a " Weak Will," may be considered, for all practical purposes, synonymous. A defect in Mind is also a defect in Will. To remedy the one is to benefit the other. The Will, equally with all the powers of the Mind, can be developed by exercise—employment, use. The muscles of the arms of a clerk do not compare with those of the engineer, blacksmith, or trained athlete. You may safely conclude — making due allowances for temperament, etc.—that the want of muscular power in the clerk is due to want of physical exercise, while the possession of muscular power and fitness in the engineer or athlete is due to exercise— employment, use. In the former the deterioration is due to neglect, and in the latter the fitness is due to exercise. Now apply the illustration to the cultivation or the neglect of the Will, and you possess the Key to the whole matter.

The Will is weak, just as certain faculties of the Mind are weak, and strong where they are strong. All men—except idiots and the weak-minded—have the power to Will and to Do. Even those who talk of having weak Wills *are merely making excuses for doing something which they would rather do, and for avoiding something else for which they have no taste or interest. If they won't do, they can refrain from doing, which shows they have a Will and exercise it in the way they choose.* The difference between the man of weak Will so-called and the man of sense exercising his intelligence is this: the former is willing to let things go; to follow the lines of the least resistance in the gratification of whatever emotion, passion, appetite, or desire may be most active in his nature (regardless of whether such gratification be good or bad), so long as he gets enjoyment out of it for the time being. When things turn out badly under these conditions, as they generally do, he says, " I could not help myself, my Will is so weak." This is a cowardly employment of self - deception; however defective he may have been in morality, and in spirituality, he is not defective in Will. He Wills to do wrong, and does it in whatever direction his inclinations are the strongest.

Please find out your weak and your strong points and do not deceive yourself into saying, " MY WILL IS WEAK," when you really mean that you have been gratifying the propensities, the emotions, and passions, rather than exercising the intellect—tempered by the moral and spiritual sentiments—to do those things which you know would be more creditable. You have instead been saying and doing foolish things, because you have found that easier than to restrain and control yourself. Increase your knowledge of yourself, by calm reflection on your own past experiences; let there be sincere convictions as to what is most necessary to your life that you may become a true man—a being worthy of the name of man—and the Will to do wrong will soon become the WILL TO DO RIGHT. YOU WILL DO RIGHT BECAUSE YOU HAVE SO DECIDED.

It may be true that a long course of self-gratification has brought about certain habits which have become more or less automatic, and not so readily mastered at first. If convictions of wrong have been aroused, and the consciousness, intellectual and moral, convincing you that a change is requisite is borne in upon you, the true battle of manhood has dawned—these habits have to be fought, and the Will educated or strengthened on the lines of the struggle to that end. Your mental muscles where weak are to be strengthened by exercise; new exertions are to be made, and you are making them. Instead of floating on the stream in the indulgence of some strongly aroused emotion —easily excited because often aroused—you now strike out; stand up against the stream of habit, feebly, probably, at first, but resolutely strike out, and with the change of direction bringing other mental muscles into play, you acquire strength as you go along, and as the power of the habit or habits becomes less and less, you become more and more MASTER OF YOURSELF.

The Will may be simple or compound, generally the latter. Desire is not Will. Motive is not Will, neither is choice. There are so many distinct mental operations which—like love, hate, covetousness, vanity, conceit, suspicion, benevolence, moral and intellectual refinement—may be behind or in the wish *to do*, but are not in themselves the executive function of the Mind, which is the Will. To use the language of Gall:—

"Will is not an impulse resulting from the activity of a single organ, or, according to certain authors, the mere feeling of desire. In order that a man may not so limit himself to wishing so that he may Will, the concurrent activity of several of the higher intellectual faculties is necessary; motives must be weighed, compared, judged. The decision resulting from this operation is called Will."

A simple illustration will help to make this clearer.

"A child is in a garden and sees delicious clusters of grapes within reach. Appetite suggests their desirability, and he plucks some and eats. The owner finds him eating the grapes and chastises him for eating the grapes. Later the child goes into the garden and sees the fruit again. His appetite is aroused again and he would gladly help himself. He then goes to his mother and tells her that he has seen some nice grapes in a garden and he wants some, but the owner will whip him if he takes any. The mother tells him it is wrong to take them, because they are the property of another. But, perhaps, if he will go and ask the owner for some, they will be given to him. He immediately acts in accordance with her advice and gets some of the desired fruit."

In the foregoing you see both the simple and the combined sources of the Will. The simple and impelling source has its basis in the appetite, and this has been aroused by the sight of the objects desired or lusted for. Covetousness comes into play; theft follows. Further, we see other factors coming in. Cautiousness has been aroused by punishment, and this brings restraint. The mother inculcates honesty—the right and the wrong of it — and then follows both self-restraint and self-respect. Under guidance courtesy takes the place of theft, want of self - respect, and dishonesty.

Take the foregoing home, and you will see that the WILL is not less strong, but it has been educated—that is to say, the mind, the intellect, has been improved. Substitute any other mental power for appetite, and consider the whole matter quietly and see what bearing that has in your own life. With this ignorant child the Will was at first exercised without enlightenment or regard of consequences. With instruction a different course of action was decided on. Consequences are considered. Now that is just what you can do.

REVIEW, PONDER, WEIGH, COMPARE, AND JUDGE, AND
THEN DECIDE, IN ALL DEPARTMENTS OF LIFE, *before*
ACTION.

Do not tell me that your Will is too weak for this.
If you have ability enough to read these instructions,
you have ability to make any improvement in life
and conduct you think best. Do not merely think
about it, ACT. CARRY YOUR THINKING INTO ACTION.
Begin at the beginning. The best way to leave off
the old habit is to COMMENCE SOMETHING FRESH. The
breaking off of old habits, and the giving up of old
connections may mean hard work, if it means you
are parting with something which you would rather
cling to, but are afraid to do so. CUT YOURSELF LOOSE
AT ONCE, and you will find it easier, when you are
truly interested in the NEW AND BETTER WAYS. Lot's
wife failed when she looked back. Had she kept
looking forward, the story would have had a better
ending.

When once you are thoroughly impressed with the
necessity of saving yourself, and making the very
best of life, you will commence at once the battle
and get rid of the old habits. Don't dally; don't
tarry; don't look back; get into the NEW. Let
"Conquer or die" be your motto, and by concentrated and persistent effort you will ultimately extri-
cate yourself from all old modes and get into newer,
brighter, and better ways.

If there be any weakness of Will, that Will is
strengthened by the conscious conviction of the necessity

of *change of direction.* You are the same man, with the same qualities of head and heart, only you have decided to take another course, and as you turn your back on the past, the old habits and the old claims and chains of the past become less effective. Be certain you have fresh interests and fresh ideas, new channels of thought, OCCUPATION, and all will be well. It was only when the house was swept and garnished, and the housewife had nothing to do, that the devils with an augmented band took possession again.

The whole thing centres on change of direction. The Will is there in every man according to capacity. The immoral man, the trickster, the fast and the smart man of bounce and "Swank," shows that he has as much "Will-power" as the man who, from higher convictions, decides that all these proceedings are wrong and determines to live a staid, clean, self-reliant, circumspect, industrious, purposeful, useful, and a responsible life, sweetened with moral respect for the good and well-being of his fellows.

There are hereditary tendencies, and no two persons are alike, and all have their strong and their weak points; but these are incentives to improvement, not excuses for the lack of endeavour. Whatever the hereditary *bias* may be, there are such things as education, advancement, management, progress, GROWTH. These latter are yours.

SUCCESS IN LIFE does not mean, however useful, the acquirement and the possession of riches, but being able to adapt yourself to your relations in life ; finding the sphere for your talents, or that for which you are best adapted. Deliberately, earnestly, learn to make the best of present circumstances—whether in business or in social life—to know yourself, state of health, bias of temperament, points of strength or weakness, and avoid whatever would call into play that which you know in yourself to be the least desirable. Diligently follow that which is best in you. No time should be wasted over the impracticable. If you have no taste for music, or mechanics, and are more suitable for a business career, do not waste time with music or by spoiling good material in learning to be a mechanic, when you are better adapted for other work. That for which you are best adapted, *work for all that it is worth*. Suppose you are musical or artistic, or both, the same advice applies. Fit yourself for that for which you are best adapted. This does not exclude self-improvement—with an effort when necessary—where intellectual and moral considerations indicate the necessity.

You are in a place of responsibility; you know that your work is difficult, and, possibly, you have to deal with those who are ready to take advantage of your defects. There may also be other difficulties of which you know that may suggest "fear of failure." You will be wise to throw this fear aside and with determination proceed with your task. Master your resources; get hold of every bit of knowledge bearing on your work; *say nothing*, study quietly, and GO AHEAD—EVERY DAY GO AHEAD. And you will soon realise that you are getting an increase of power. The tasks become easier; your self-confidence is increased; what you feared was only the *fear of a fear*, and had no existence. You will meet and overcome your difficulties, one after the other. You are getting confidence in yourself. What you wish to do, you Will to do, and you do it. Instead of waiting to consult others and anxiously await their verdict, their applause, their sneers, you see what is required yourself, decide, and act. You have no forebodings, no fears; your acts speak for themselves, and your employers or your clients are satisfied; and, if not exactly influenced in your favour, they will instinctively recognise your ability, judgment, and strength.

Look at the matter straight in the light of your own experience. You will find that your WILL is strong enough in the direction of your inclinations. Even the things you are willing to do, when opportunity renders possible, you can refrain from doing, if not expedient, from sense of duty, or from any other cause. What you Will to do, you can do; and what you say you cannot do, means that it is something which you are not WILL(ing) to do.

WHAT YOU WILL TO BE YOU CAN BE.

BEGIN AT THE BEGINNING. BEGIN WITH SELF.

WHEN YOU THINK FEEBLY, YOU WILL ACT FEEBLY.

NO ONE ACTS FEEBLY WHERE TRULY INTERESTED.

WHATEVER YOU THINK IN YOUR HEART, YOU ARE.

WHAT ARE YOU? THINK RIGHT AND THE VICTORY IS YOURS.

ACT WITHOUT QUESTION ON THE HINTS GIVEN YOU.

THE GREATEST VICTORY OF ALL IS THE CONQUEST OF SELF.

IT IS THE "JUST NOW" MAN WHO ACHIEVES THAT VICTORY.

After you have gone through your Breathing Exercises, lie or sit in silence for five to ten minutes and slowly repeat to yourself these sentences. Think over them. Decide in your mind the course you have determined on. Keep the matter to yourself. Go ahead. Quietly and firmly act.

By proceeding on the lines suggested, you are already practising and are being benefited by non-comatose, auto-suggestion procedure, concerning which very simple, concise, and practical instructions will be given you later on.

CHAPTER IX

DEFECTS OF THE WILL, AND HOW TO CURE THEM

"Are you in earnest? Seize this very minute.
  Whatever you can do, or dream you can—begin it.
  Boldness has genius, power, magic in it.
  Only engage—and then the mind grows heated.
  Begin !—and then the work will be completed."

GOETHE.

IN the last lesson I dealt pretty freely with the WILL; and in this I propose to touch on some defects of the WILL, and how to remedy them. If I put the matter clearly before you, you will be all the more able to put yourself in training. I will not mention all the defects in WILL, for the simple reason that it would be impossible. I will mention some, suggest others, and you yourself will supply the rest, as far as you yourself are concerned. I teach; you train. I give you the keys; you employ them. You will know the mental cupboards you want to keep shut, and those it will be best to leave open. No amount of reading will suffice, unless you yourself put into practice that which is taught. Take time and get a free and clearly defined intellectual grasp of what I want you to do, and then DO IT, and KEEP ON DOING, until, by practice, it becomes *one*

133

with self.   There is an old and a wise saying : " It is not hearers of the word, but the doers of it shall be saved." Apply this to yourself, if you would succeed in life ; improve self, and overcome all that which hinders you.

To overcome any defect in self, or any serious diffi- culty in life; to command and direct others—in a word, to achieve SUCCESS, you must be first convinced of the necessity ; count the cost ; summon your energies and then act.   THAT WAY SUCCESS LIES.   SUCCESS IS FOR YOU AND NOT FOR THE FAINT-HEARTED AND UN- DECIDED MAN.

To roughly generalise between the Wise and the Foolish.   The Wise suffer in advance and are benefited afterwards.   The Foolish go in for what they call benefits first, and suffer subsequently.   This is an important difference, and while none are wholly wise or totally foolish, the foregoing distinction remains true, and is worthy of a little more consideration.

The Wise suffer in advance ; plan with care, weigh, consider, deny themselves—of what others call enjoy- ment, pleasure, comfort—and perhaps suffer penury, in laying the foundations of Success.   They gather up their forces, Act and *keep on doing*, with the result that Success and Happiness are theirs.   Success comes first ; Happiness follows as a result.   Even when they have not gained all that their mind had been set upon, they have reaped a greater Success than would have been possible otherwise.

The Foolish enjoy (?) first, and suffer afterwards. And I may add that the penalties which the Foolish reap are always more severe than those which fall to the lot of the Wise. The career of the Foolish—in the pursuit of what he terms enjoyment or happiness—is a menace to the well-being of others. His acts not only entail suffering on others, but dull his own intellect, hamper his progress, and take from him some measure of that refinement and sensitiveness which, rightly employed, make for worth. In consequence of this blunting of the intellect and the stupefying of the true sense of refinement, the penalties which his outraged nature must bear do not debar him from further indulgence in his folly. That is to say, as soon as he is relieved from the reaction of one piece of folly, he either repeats it or runs into something else, according to the sentiments or the propensities seeking gratification.

With the sensible man it is different. His sufferings are compensatory. They direct him. They do not dull the intellect or blunt his sensibilities. His sufferings are twofold, those which he brings on himself and those which are entailed upon him. The former are voluntary, such as denying himself; facing what he must lose, if he decides to follow the path which his moral and spiritual leanings and his intellect have decided as the only worthy and sensible course for him to pursue. Then there are penalties which even the wisest man cannot escape—as none are perfect— and which they suffer in consequence of errors in judgment. But even these are blessings in disguise. They do no real harm. They benefit. For the experiences which they bring assist him as to future action. He acts with greater prudence and with more decision and force when the time comes.

I will take for granted that you are the wise man, or mean to be to the very best of your own awakened enlightenment; also that you realise to some extent that the foregoing picture is true, although you find that you have not only to pay for errors in judgment, but that you suffer too from the follies and the malice of others. You may even lose friendships which you cherish, and you may have to face other trials which test your faith and patience. In all these things there is compensation. If you are afflicted, let it be in the path of duty—living your best and most healthy life —and not in the neglect of it. Having made up your mind as to the course you, at least, mean to pursue, go on, neither turning to the left nor the right. Act in accordance with the decision at which you have arrived, seeking neither praise nor fearing censure. Be a MAN, not a reed shaken by the wind. Know your own Mind and obey it, and you will have your reward and happiness in a sweeter and happier life. In other words, you are using your WILL in order to get the most out of life, or the most good out of yourself—your faculties— out of your own special spheres of labour, mastering your difficulties therein as well as the defects in yourself, knowing that you will ASSUREDLY REAP THAT FOR WHICH YOU WORK.

The foolish or short-sighted man, whether he works or plays or loafs, reaps equally and as certainly that for which he has lived. For instance, he believes in taking it easy; in having a good time (?); in being social, "hale fellow, well met"—whether at his own expense or that of others—and he has all these things for a time. He is not to be "tied in" by what he calls "Puritanical hypocrisy," which you will recognise as merely sobriety, cleanliness in life, and thoughtful consideration for others. It matters little if he suffers from the head of the drinker in the morning or from the heavier and the graver penalties which follow the violation of the inherent laws of man's constitution— that head and those penalties have been worked for, just as certainly as the more desirable benefits for which you are now working, and all the good for which you have worked.

You are employing your WILL, which is the sum of the Intellect—sustained by the Moral and Spiritual forces of the mind—and the other is using his WILL— his Intellect—*subordinated* to his emotions, passions, animal propensities, and REAPS WHAT HE HAS SOWN.

Both the Wise and the Foolish exercise WILL-POWER, but with a difference as to quality and motive. The former thinks in advance, directs his course, and has a greater measure of Success in consequence. He is recognised as trustworthy, honourable, and reliable. The latter has no such reputation. He is expedient, and has no higher guiding principle than the service of self. He is perhaps clever, tricky, and wide-awake— or thinks himself to be so. Takes an advantage now, regardless of the right or the wrong of it, so long as he is gratified. Boasts that "a bird in the hand is worth two in the bush." And he may boom for a time, but when the reckoning comes, as it always does, bankruptcy of mind, body, and estate are his. Although it is not as bad as this, and there is what is called "estate" left, the receivers are seldom really benefited thereby.

Be ye Wise or Foolish, there is no way of getting away from the fact—

WHATEVER A MAN THINKETH IN HIS HEART HE IS.

HE ACTS AS HE REALLY THINKS—NOT WHAT HE ASSUMES TO THINK.

HE ADVANCES AS HE THINKS ARIGHT, and HE DETERIORATES AS HE THINKS WRONGLY.

HE IS WHATEVER HIS THOUGHT MAKES HIM.

You have the shaping of your attitude of Mind. You will have no difficulty in deciding the course to pursue. You will develop and educate the WILL by which you will discount trouble, avert difficulties, overcome obstacles, govern yourself, and even control your environment. You can of course take no special pains and let your undisciplined WILL have its way, so that you can get "square" when you feel that way; speak when your dignity is offended; write letters when angry; be impulsive and jump to conclusions and act—not on the merits of the case—but because some-one has rubbed up against your grain and made you feel sore. Perhaps you will go further and plow the sands of your appetites, just to show that you won't be dictated to, and make a fool of yourself.

You see quite clearly that it is within your power to choose and follow either of the foregoing courses. No, you will not select the last course. Perhaps not definitely select it. There is hope in that. Unless one is watchful, it is possible to drift into it. As the telling of one lie leads to another, so the gratification of one desire leads to either that of another or to the repetition of the first, and so drift on into the "down grade." No, you will not select that course. And if you have been drifting or suspect now that you are not watchful enough, take command of yourself at once. Keep a clear look-out, with your hand firmly on the helm of your ship of life. Steer a definite course for a definite end. Keep at it. There may be strong and there may be cross currents, adverse winds; something of discomfort, and now and then a cold douche. What of the one or the other? These things will only harden you. Keep to your course. A safe haven and peace are yours.

You are a person of good intellect and therefore possess a good WILL. The Intellectual Faculties, whose centres are in the prefrontal lobes of the brain, enable you to perceive persons, objects, and things, their qualities and relations. When these qualities act together they constitute the true WILL. *Will therefore is as is the Intellect.* It is as strong as certain faculties and as weak as others are.

The boy's WILL, being the outcome of his perceptive powers, and stimulated by aroused emotions, will lack something which the more matured Will of man possesses. The latter is, or ought to be, the outcome of superior powers of perception, aided by the increased experience of the Knowing faculties, and enhanced by man's superior powers of reflection, reason, or judgment. Man's WILL should be further increased by the consciousness of his own relation to persons and to his environment, by whom and by which he may be influenced, and on whom and by which he may exercise his WILL. Rightly considered, the WILL is the Intellect and the Intellect is the WILL.

To improve the WILL, improve the Intellect—in other words, that which is called "Mind." You are sufficiently acquainted with the imperfections of Human Nature to know—what a very cursory view of morals and society will confirm—that the Intellect is the most dominant factor—at least it should be— in the Human Mind, and this Intellect is too often overshadowed by the passions and the appetites, and that therefore as a consequence deeds are committed which are detrimental to the welfare of the individual and society. And they are done at the time, just as much by the WILL of the doer, as the more meritorious things are accomplished in his wiser and saner moments.

You know that hasty deeds are to be regretted for a variety of reasons, and you have observed that A SINGLE ACT OF FOLLY HAS OFTEN OVERSHADOWED A LIFE.

Examine yourself. Wherein is your WILL weak? A fort is not so much defended by keeping an eye on the enemy and resisting his attacks, as by making sure that the fort itself is all right; that its weak points have been looked after and strengthened ; and that each member of the garrison, according to his rank and position, obeys the orders issued by the commander. So with yourself, while not by any means neglecting the enemy—external things, adverse conditions, and environment — look after the subordinates of the Intellect, the WILL, the moral and the religious forces, the executive powers, the affections, the appetites and passions. See that they do your bidding, keep their place, fight, or keep sentry, or whatever else is required of them—they must be obedient to orders.

You may have a strong WILL and yet be colour blind, or perhaps be deficient in order. Well, so far as these are concerned your WILL will be weak. In the first, no amount of desire—willing—will make you able to distinguish colours, as the defect is due to organic deficiency in the cerebral centre of colour. Your lack of order may be susceptible of improvement, because the cerebral centre or organ is not so defective as that of colour-vision. By giving attention to details, by making a point to have a place for everything and making a mental note of that, your order will improve. In the matter of order your WILL is strengthened ; in that of colour it is not. In the power of appreciating colours the Intellect is that of an idiot and non-existent. These two illustrations are extreme, but they serve to suggest what can be improved and what it would be a waste of time to attempt to improve.

The man with one talent has generally but little desire to use it. He is ready to make excuses for its neglect or non-employment. *He has little interest that way.* Those with three, five, or ten talents have greater incentives to employ what they have, and their reward is proportionate to their diligence. In a word, *where there is no interest, there is no desire.* Where there is interest you may conclude there is capacity—a real something to be educated and employed. Where there is the interest, you have the intellect—THE WILL and the ABILITY and the POWER for SELF-CULTURE AND IMPROVEMENT.

As the Intellectual Faculties—which perceive relations and form Ideas—constitute the WILL, the affective faculties and the propensities execute the commands of the WILL. Whether the desire is noble or ignoble, it is the WILL which makes the choice. The Intellect may perceive the right relations and the proper mode of action and the time to act; the moral sentiments the right and the wrong of it. If there be sufficient grit and courage in your composition, that which you have determined on you will carry out.

Sometimes there may not be so much lack of WILL, as some weakness in the executive powers of the WILL. That is to say, one may not be lacking—in any essential degree—in one single faculty of the Intellect, but appears unable—until educated—to carry out the behests of the WILL, from some weakness—real or imaginary—in one's executive powers. Thus there may be a lack of Firmness or Courage, or one may have an excess of Cautiousness, which gives timidity, and there may be a certain amount of temperamental shyness, nervousness, and lack of health, which suggests want of *grit* or staying power. But all these defects can be remedied. Encourage no weakness, and utilise to the best advantage whatever is in you that is best. All the faculties of the mind can be developed by exercise. Whatever is defective, or moderately so, in the executive faculties, can be improved by you. You are not a man of one talent. You are intelligent, have interests; direct your forces and go ahead. *You must realise as a fact in experience that you always do better when you try.* That which you often imagined to be an obstacle, faded away before you when you aroused yourself into action.

The bully—who is almost always a coward—can, when occasion demands it, work himself up into a fury in order to carry out the behests of his ill-formed WILL. The whisky bottle often supplies him with "Dutch courage," or with recklessness, which he ignorantly confounds with courage, and then he attempts to carry out that which he has decided to do. All such methods are rejected by the man of sense, who takes time to think. Knowing his own mind and having ascertained what he really WILLS to have done, by the conscious direction and right consideration of all the motives and of the end in view to be attained, sets in operation the Executive forces of the WILL—Firmness, Self-esteem, Continuity, Combativeness, and even Destructiveness—to carry out the behests and decisions of the Intellect, which is his WILL.

Thus you will see, following the choice and the decision of the Mind comes the question of execution or performance. It is your duty to know yourself—in the light of your own past personal experience, and, where necessary, aided by the opinion of a Character-reading Expert—and consider well that for which you are best fitted. If you are not in your groove, either get into it or MAKE IT. Work on these lines; throw yourself into that work, heart and soul. Where your interest lies there will your heart be. For good or ill, this is true of the human race and will be true of you. Your energy, pluck, and determination will respond to the interest. Concentration and perseverance are essential. Be firm and these will come all right. Energy, pluck, and enthusiasm will do a great deal, but supported by patience and perseverance will accomplish more.

STEADY PERSEVERANCE spells SUCCESS. It is not the spurt for the moment that makes for Success. It is the quiet, steady plod, the repeated endeavour that wins. You cultivate Firmness and Concentration by so doing. Do you want a little more ? What is it ? Tell me. You can overcome most difficulties by bringing a little more pre-thought, method, and arrangement into your life and work. Thus you will save time and accomplish more. The difficulties to be faced and mastered in that in which you are most interested will be worked out with greater Success, because you will approach your task with greater courage, executive skill; with more cheerfulness and hopeful patience, and in a concentrated, orderly, and consecutive manner. Whatever you do, BE FULLY PERSUADED IN YOUR OWN MIND, AND THEN, WHAT- EVER YOUR HANDS FIND TO DO, THAT DO WITH ALL YOUR MIGHT.

There are not only defects in WILL but in the execu- tion of the WILL to be guarded against. There are primal desires which arise from large and active propensities, or from some outward stimuli which may have a similar effect upon them. Individual instances need not be pointed out. As the sight of the grapes aroused the desire of the child for possession, so every other propensity and power or faculty can be aroused. Fostered, the gratification becomes a habit. Whether the habit be good or evil is a matter which can only be determined on its merits. Some have inherited un- desirable habits or tendencies thereto, but these—what- ever their nature—are not without remedy. Where there is intelligence to recognise the defect and appreciate the necessity for reform, all difficulties, in due time, CAN and WILL BE OVERCOME.

Of two errors of Will in my opinion most common, is that one in which a tendency is shown of *under- estimating* oneself. The other that of over-estimating. The first is a real and a serious drawback. Neither are desirable. *What is wanted is real confidence, arising from a correct knowledge of oneself.* The errors of under- estimation can never be fully gauged. Science, art, literature, mechanics, professional work, commerce, social and private life, have all suffered in consequence of this *under-estimation* and *self-consciousness.* The good which could have been done has been left undone, and much misery and unhappiness entailed on self and others in consequence of this want of Self-reliance.

WHATEVER YOU DO, KNOW YOURSELF, BELIEVE IN YOUR-SELF, AND PUT ALL THAT YOU KNOW IS BEST IN YOURSELF INTO YOUR LIFE AND WORK. This is true Self-reliance in practice.

Over-estimation corrects itself. The over-confident individual who cannot confirm his confidence with "good works" is seldom taken at his own valuation and is sure to find his true level. The world is very shrewd, and will take you and I not at our own apprisement, or what we say of ourselves or proclaim we can do, but for what we have been able to achieve. *Show a clean record, have faith in yourself, and help will follow.*

Defeat is distressing to weak minds—self-apprised at too high a value—those who court flattery, wheedle and manœuvre for applause, and fail to command them. Defeat is not a cause of repining to the intelligent or strong-willed. These latter set about diligently to re-examine the ground, and ascertain the cause or causes of their defeat; profit by the real or apparent disaster and get to work again, and, if need be, again and again, and SUCCEED.

In this spirit tackle yourself—for the causes of defeat or success lie largely in yourself. Tackle the problems of life, and work which lies nearest to you and your WILL will grow and you will develop a worthy man-hood, an intelligent masterfulness—WILL-POWER and SUCCESS are yours.

HAVE FAITH IN YOURSELF, PUT THAT AND YOUR BEST INTO WORK; CONCENTRATE, AND DO ONE THING AT A TIME.

HAVE FAITH IN YOURSELF AND TAKE PLEASURE IN YOUR WORK, AND, WHATEVER YOU DO, SHOW THAT YOU CAN DO IT AND DO IT THOROUGHLY.

HAVE FAITH IN YOURSELF AND KEEP YOURSELF FIT AND CHEERFUL, AND WHAT IS TO BE DONE, DO WITH DETERMINATION TO THE BEST OF YOUR ABILITY.

HAVE FAITH IN YOURSELF, and, if you are an employee, SEE HOW MUCH YOU CAN DO AND PUT INTO YOUR WORK, and NOT HOW LITTLE.

HAVE FAITH IN YOURSELF; MAGNIFY YOUR OFFICE; ENNOBLE YOUR WORK, AND YOUR WORK WILL ENNOBLE AND DIGNIFY YOU.

And lastly—

HAVE FAITH IN YOURSELF IN ALL THAT YOU DO. NEVER SPEAK WHEN YOU CAN ACHIEVE YOUR END WITHOUT IT; NEVER WRITE WHEN YOU CAN SEE AND INTERVIEW. IF YOU MUST WRITE, WRITE AS YOU WOULD SPEAK. SAY NOTHING WITHOUT A PURPOSE, AND WHETHER SILENT, SPEAKING, OR WRITING, PUT COURTESY, CHEERFULNESS, AND SELF-RELIANCE INTO ALL THAT YOU DO. HAVE FAITH IN YOURSELF, AND OTHERS WILL HAVE FAITH IN YOU. NEVER SAY "I CAN'T," WITHOUT HONESTLY DOING THE "I CAN."

Frequently repeat the foregoing sentences—in the first person—and picture out to yourself the advantages which will accrue to you through having greater faith in yourself.

CHAPTER X

"To me the man hardly seems to be free, who does not sometimes do nothing."—CICERO.

IN proceeding with this lesson, I pause a moment to repeat, "Tone of Mind depends on vigour of organisation." That is a proposition which few will deny. Mind is here recognised as something distinct from the body, and yet depending on the vigour and health of the body, and of the Mind's essential instruments—the brain and the nervous system — for its tone and manifestation.

It is also true—which a little experience in life has made clear to you—that there have been and are many instances of persons possessing, with feebleness of body and with old age, great clearness and ability of Mind. But these are the exceptions which prove the rule that "Tone of Mind depends on vigour of Organisation." In looking into the history of these exceptional cases, it will be found that these persons were in the heyday of life more remarkable still for the power, the vigour, and the ascendency of their Minds—their power to lead, influence, and control their fellows by speech and

148

by pen—through their Magnetic Personality. It will also be found that with old age and a feeble body there was something lacking, namely, " Continuity of power," and although there was and might be flashes of former power and ability, there was a lack of mental staying power. Lacking this Continuity—this staying power and connectedness of thought—in the former masterly degree, the power and the brilliancy which once made their name famous was no longer theirs.

It may not be your lot to be either great or famous, but it is yours to be greater and much more able to succeed in the battle of life than hitherto, by

(a) Living a healthy, temperate life, and

(b) By cultivating this " Continuity of power."

By following out faithfully the hints given in these lessons, you will be able to preserve your health—cultivate the "vigour of Organisation." And by the discipline of thought, and the conscious direction of your thinking; by the exercise of Will-power—Perseverance, Patience, Order—with a quiet and steady Firmness, you will attain that "continuity of power" and tone of Mind which make for Success.

Whatever Mind is in its essential self, it is sufficient for you to know or be conscious of the fact that you have a Mind, and that you have learned in connection with your own experiences something of the power and the vigour and the Mastery of thought. Leave all matters relating to the discussion as to the essential nature of Mind to the metaphysician and the psychologist,—you will not have time for that now. It is sufficient for you to know that in this life—with which we are most familiar, and yet about which we are so inadequately informed—we know of no Mind apart from organisation ; and so, whatever Mind is in itself, we know that its power and force is affected by many conditions peculiar to this life, such as the state of the body—especially of the brain and the nervous system —that is, on the health and integrity of its physical instruments—by which and through which the mental powers or the Mind are manifested in this life.

You will have observed that if one or more of the organs of sense are diseased, imperfect, the Mind will be so far imperfectly informed of that which is taking place in the world without ; or if by ignorance, or perhaps worse, the life lived has had a devitalising effect on the system, the brain—especially the pre-frontal region— will be more or less exhausted ; and, owing to the brain being inadequately nourished on the one hand, and unduly exhausted on the other, the Intellectual powers of the Mind cannot be adequately manifested.

As you desire to succeed in life, commence to-day to conserve your vital powers, and, if possible, improve them. That you can improve them will soon be demonstrated. When I tell you to conserve your vital powers, I do not mean you to be lazy or afraid to put out energy when necessary ; but—and I have enjoined silence in a former lesson—I mean you to save or conserve your vital powers, by refraining from unnecessary talk, work, restless movements, worries, and anxieties, which serve no useful purpose. I do not mean either by conserving your vital powers, that you are to leave anything to anybody which you should do yourself ; but I do mean that you should not fritter away your time and energy in doing things which could as well be done by subordinates. In no sense depend on others to accomplish for you that which you can accomplish yourself; do not depend on persons, foods, drugs, and have anxieties concerning the preservation and improvement of your health and vigour of organisation. Simply learn what MODERATION MEANS, and live a clean, temperate, sensible life, and the desired Vigour of Organisation will be yours.

Personal Magnetism and the development of Will-power are yours, on the lines which I have marked out. Preserve what health you have and increase it by judicious living, or by the exercise of a sadly neglected virtue—in these days of gush, push, self-advertisement, and competition—viz. MODERATION.

By the exercise of Moderation, you will be able to make the most of your opportunities. Whether they come but once or several times, make use of them and you will have time enough to grow in grace and in strength for the performance of the longest and the hardest duties, but *no time* to engage in the shortest follies or worse.

Moderation is temperance in all things which are good, and the total avoidance of that which is evil, whether that evil be the thinking of evil, the harbouring of vanity, of FEAR, of vice, of folly, or that which arises from erroneous habits in eating and drinking. These latter habits are a pregnant source of evil, and are indulged in by many good men and women too, who would be esteemed as persons of unspotted character. These evil habits of eating and drinking—while not by any means those of gluttony and drunkenness—do more than anything else, in my opinion, to sap the foundations of health, and hinder the true development of man in self-control, and all that means in the manifestation of Mind. As to the correct modes of eating and drinking, a few hints will be given.

Success comes to him who labours for it, but he has to labour with judgment. Not to the man who is always doing, who is up late and early, who has no time to rest, as his services are so important to himself or to the world—lest Time should get out of joint and the World go wrong—and so burns the candle of life at both ends, and makes a mess of it. This incessant worker goes to the wall, and Time and the World somehow get on without him. Possibly you have met such—I meet these people every day. They are always doing; always suffering; over-anxious; exhausted; anæmic in brain, or, perhaps, more or less congested. They suffer from brain-fag and discover that they are victims of *neurasthenia*. They know that, because they have read a book which told them so. They go from bad to worse. They try a little spirits; are distressed about their food, vary that, and then take this medicine and that. They take the medicines which have done wonders—for other people—so the advertisements read. They are so sensitive, nervous, and so good, that they have tried everything—too much of many things, in fact, and they are still afflicted—except MODERATION.

Well, take a lesson from this. Are you out of sorts? Is the brain machinery run down a little? Try MODERATION as a remedy, and you will find that without nine-tenths of the outlay in time, money, and in nervous energy, you will avoid the greater share of the troubles of which they complain, and presently remove those from which you suffer. A little restraint, a little exercise of the WILL over the emotions, passions, appetites—in a word, exercise MODERATION and ALL WILL BE WELL.

You will find in the following some inexpensive methods by which MODERATION can be exercised with great advantage to yourself. An old-time prophet wisely said: "There is a time for all things." And for our purpose, let us say, that success in life comes as much from NOT doing as in doing. We—you—are made for rest as well as for work. MODERATION has to be applied to the one as well as to the other. The always-must-be-doing man fires himself out of the world, just as readily as the loafer who corrupts and rusts himself out. Let these take their way, but it is not to be your way. *Yours is to be a moderate, temperate, and sensible life. Work while working; play when playing;* REST *when resting.* Let the work be done when it has to be done. Rest whenever Nature indicates that to be necessary, but do not mix work, rest, and play. One thing at a time. Give each their place and their time. Even if you have but scant time for play—enjoyment in the lighter duties and social side of life —do not under any circumstances deprive yourself of REST. Your length of days, at best, are short, but you can lengthen them considerably by resting as conscientiously as you work. Throw yourself cheerfully into both, and you will be wise.

However hard you have got to work, you will be all the fitter for it by having healthful rest. Not to-morrow, not when you retire, or are pensioned, or in eternity, but just now, to-day, and in each and every day in right proportion.

REST, mental rest, is sometimes to be obtained by change of occupation; thus, a financier heavily engaged in abstruse calculations all day may find mental rest in reading a light magazine article, while the calculating centres of the brain are resting. A change of occupation does help, but that can never take the place of real rest. Rest in its place is essential to success. Your brain needs rest to recuperate. Your stomach requires it. The lungs demand it, and the muscles of the body—if not the whole body—need their proportion of rest, and you must see that they get it. The brain, or mental engine, especially needs rest, cleaning up, renovating; and this self-adjustment mainly takes place in sleep. Your brain will work all the better in your waking moments for that rest. An ordinary locomotive requires rest, cleaning up, and rectifying, and great care is expended in this way, so that its running and racing may be successful. The brain is the most delicate vital machine in the human organisation. All the other organs of the body are in a measure subservient to its necessities. When the brain is properly rested and nurtured, life's work runs in a comparatively smooth and easy manner.

REST.—The first essential is Brain Rest. The amount of rest required will depend on both your temperament and work. The best rest is that which Nature automatically furnishes—SLEEP. Although I have already referred to sleep, a few more remarks will not be out of place. It is during sleep that the brain —including the whole nervous structure of man—is re-adjusted, restored, or recuperated. It is positively suicidal to rob yourself of sufficient sleep. You will find it a good thing when you lie down at night to let all care, business worries, anxieties, and all wake-a-day responsibilities and duties *Go*. GO TO BED TO SLEEP AND NOT TO THINK. LET EVERYTHING GO. LET EVERY-THING GO, AND SLEEP. Nature demands it. Your head will be all the brighter and the clearer for the work, the duties, the love and the companionship which the daylight brings, and from which no honest man or woman need shrink. The day is for active work or thought and work ; the night for sleep. Let your brain be adequately rested and you will handle all your difficulties all the better. You will be able to face them and overcome them. It is possible to go without food for a week, a month, or six weeks, but you cannot do without sleep. It is imperative that you have, at the very least, six hours' sleep in the twenty-four.

Without this a serious break-down in the mental machinery may be looked for, if not a premature shortening of your career. Occasions may arise when you may have to deprive yourself of a night's rest; but to do so by lying thinking over your real or imaginary woes, or to take advantage of your fellows, or to spend your substance in the gratification of desire, is absolutely criminal and a sin against your constitution. Also an unhealthy attitude of mind which courts defeat and a violation of Nature's laws—for this you will have to pay the uttermost farthing.

Let MODERATION be your guiding star, in this as in all other matters. Do not foolishly prolong your hours in bed and waste your opportunities. When Fortune comes round and finds you in bed, when you should be up and doing, she will pass on and extend her invitations and her confidences to your neighbour, who is awake and ready to receive her.

Although I repeat myself, let me emphasise the importance of sleep. Do not cheat yourself of the requisite amount. Sleep in a well-ventilated room. Lie down, close your eyes, relax every muscle; take up the most comfortable position; commit your body to the care of your SOUL and the Infinite, and then LET EVERYTHING GO, and SLEEP.

If SLEEP be laggard, court it. Let your thinking reach its lowest ebb. If not, reduce the activities of the Mind by deliberately closing the eyelids, turning the eyes slightly upwards under the eyelids, and indulge in slow, soft breathing—with or without Auto-suggestions of sleep—and you will secure sleep. *In this, as in all other things, the attitude of Mind is all-important.* If you want sleep, put yourself in the way of it and you will get it just as surely as the man who does not get sleep, who keeps saying to and convincing himself, "I cannot sleep. I do not sleep. I have had such a restless night. I tried, you know, but there is no use trying." Well, the man who thinks there is no use trying—whether in sleep or in anything else—generally gets it that way, and somebody else has to bear the burden of his complaints and mental slovenliness, and without much benefit to him either. You make up your mind, when the hour for sleep comes, you are going to have it. GO TO BED TO SLEEP, NOT TO THINK, AND YOU WILL SLEEP. Where there is much to think about, you will think about it all the better next day after a good night's sleep: As the day has its work, so has the night, and in the constitution of things that is the time to sleep. There are other methods of brain recuperation and rest, but the most important of these is SLEEP. Auto-suggestions for sleep will be given later on.

REST.—The next most essential mode is STOMACH REST. With the majority of human beings, any kind of rest to the stomach is denied. The brain powers are unduly exhausted or stimulated, and the whole foundation of health sapped by carelessness and prodigality in this respect. From childhood to the grave the stomach is stuffed, pampered, and abused. And while the whole system is getting imperfect rest because of this, the stomach is getting none, and is jaded, and with its owner returns to the waking hours to be further loaded, scalded, chilled, stimulated, and further exhausted. Very few persons—as far as the stomach is concerned—understand what healthy MODERATION means. Too many, it is true, do not get enough to eat, but they are fewer in number than those who eat too much and who exercise little or no judgment in what they eat. To pamper and gratify the palate is their only aim. The aristocratic Johnny, who swills champagne and bathes in it, has glimmerings at times that he is a fool; but there are thousands of the well-to-do and respectable, over-eating and sleeping, who have no idea that they are fools at all. There are fools and fools, and these ignorant, self-satisfied ones are among the greatest.

A tired man has a tired stomach. No one should eat when they are tired. The body needs rest then, and the stomach is unfit for its work. Let it rest too, and it will do its work all the better when a light meal can be partaken with safety.

There is great folly in taking more food than necessary, and also in taking food on the top of food already lying in the stomach—the remains of a previously taken meal—in a partly digested condition. This needless burdening of the stomach is a woeful waste of vital energy. Apart from what are called stomach troubles, may be added heart derangements, headaches, irritable tempers, and the out-of-the-way excuses which many make for injudicious behaviour—there is a constant drain and perversion of the vital forces, drawn from the brain and diverted by the arterial and nervous circulation to the stomach, to enable it to do its work. The brain is jaded ; the mental powers are sluggish ; there is a tendency to sleep after a meal, or some other perversion. But why continue the picture ? Medicine flourishes on it; the manufacturers of pills and nostrums make fortunes ; Morals and Society suffer because the majority will not or cannot control their appetites. ONE OUNCE OF FOOD MORE THAN NECESSARY MEANS THE FURTHER DEPLETION OF THE VITAL AND NERVOUS ENERGIES, AND ENCUMBERS THE BODY WITH DISEASED AND USELESS MATTER. THE MENTAL MACHINERY BECOMES CLOGGED AND WILL NOT WORK. Why take that ounce, then ?

As an exercise of personal WILL-POWER, control your appetite. Practise the virtue of Moderation. Apply the virtue of MODERATION to eating and drinking so that the stomach has no more work to do than is necessary to keep the system supplied with a fair amount of recuperative nutrition. Thousands who find that this food and that food do not agree with them, and who fly to tonics, vegetarianism, patent foods, or to some other food fad or hobby, would remedy the whole trouble by the exercise of MODERA-TION.

Let me give you a few Health hints easy to remember :—

First.—Eat what you like and drink what you please —that which you have found to be good from your ex-

perience—in MODERATION.   Never eat to satiety.
Better rise from the table with the inclination to eat
more, than to rise with a sigh of sufficiency.

Second.—Never eat when tired.   A tired man has a
tired stomach.   Better rest a bit.   Have a refreshing
wash, but in any case rest before eating, when tired.

Third.—Never take stimulants, tea, coffee, and especially alcohol, to stimulate the appetite, and to wash
improperly masticated food out of the mouth into the
stomach.

Fourth.—Do not throw on the stomach the work
which should be done by the teeth.   The bolting of food
—from ignorance, *habit*, business hurry, or other causes
—means not only overloading the stomach, but with
material in a state the stomach was never intended to
operate on.

Fifth.—" He who would live long must masticate
slowly."   Let your mouthfuls be small.   Thoroughly
chew each mouthful, chewing and chewing, till each
" bit " is reduced to a pulp before swallowing.   The
appetite will be satisfied with less food, and the food
partaken will do more good.   The late Sir Andrew
Clark, Physician to Her Late Majesty, Queen Victoria,
used to press upon his dyspeptic patients that each
morsel of food required forty to fifty bites.   One might
add that there would be no dyspeptic patients if
people ate in MODERATION and CHEWED THEIR FOOD
PROPERLY.

Sixth.—Never eat because the bell rings or to oblige
a friend, or to taste the good things provided by wife,

landlady, or cook. Eat when hungry only. If you have no appetite, wait for it.

Seventh.—Let there be at least five to six hours between each meal, so that the stomach may have a short period of rest between one meal and another. Better postpone a meal than eat when there still lies in the stomach the remains of a meal taken some time previously.

Eighth.—Let all meals be eaten cheerfully, in good spirits. All topics, such as personal criticisms, business failures, diseases, the sins and shortcomings of the sinner over the way, and especially all subjects which are likely to bring about angry recriminations, or which may be opposed to good fellowship, should be rigidly excluded from the table, as indeed they should be from all decent society.

Ninth.—When conversation at the table takes the unhappy turn, either ignore it, or, what is better still, lead those present to a change of subject. If you have sense to control your appetite, you will have tact and grace enough to do that. Bread eaten in sorrow or anger, as well as food washed down with liquids, deranges the stomach and manufactures dyspeptics.

Tenth.—Let twelve hours—fifteen would be better—elapse between the last meal at night and the first in the morning. A light breakfast makes a cheerful day. When in doubt whether to eat or not to eat, it is best not to eat.

It is wise to suit one's diet to one's condition. What will do for a sedentary life will not serve for an active, laborious state of existence. I do not believe in fad diets, such as advocated by vegetarians, fruitarians, or by the beef and beer variety. I think, from the history of mankind, and from the nature of man's organisation, he is adapted to a mixed dietary. And the nations which produce the most vigorous, energetic, intellectual, and most dependable or moral types of men are those nations which use a mixed dietary of fruits, vegetables, fish and animal food. Faddists may live on cabbage and oil if they like, but I will have none of it. It is my opinion, however, that in this country we eat far too much animal food and not enough of the " kindly fruits of the earth," in their appropriate season. We use too much white bread, from which the most nourishing qualities are extracted in the manufacture and fining of the flour. We indulge too freely in condensed and artificial abominations, in which grease, sugar, and stale eggs are the principal ingredients, employed by un-principled bakers to *please* the palate.

There is, however, great folly in being pernickety about food. For example, to be in great distress because somebody will eat eels and pike, which we cannot endure the sight of; or to refuse to eat, although hungry, a nicely cooked lamb chop, because we would be accessory—after the act—to the lamb's death; maintain that we should not eat food which necessitates the taking of life, etc. But even though we lived on cabbage and its endless varieties, we could not do so without taking or partaking of its life. As a matter of fact, we cannot take a drink of water without taking life; or clean one's teeth, without that operation

being death to something. Sentiment is all right in
its place, but sentiment is overdone when it hinders
the use of suitable diet, and places a *fear fence* around
one to inhibit good sense, and forbid that good digestion
should wait on appetite.

Exclusive diets are a mistake. Vegetarians may
enjoy life in their own way, and flourish in Turkey,
Asia Minor, India, and other countries; but in the
temperate and arctic zones, a diet which excludes
animal food and animal products is a mistake. The
man who takes milk, eggs, and cheese is not one who
is a true vegetarian, and when he calls himself one is
either suffering from Self-deception, or is a bit of a
fraud. He reminds me of the teetotaler who drinks
claret, British wines, and lime juice, containing from 5
to 15 per cent. of alcohol, because they are teetotal
drinks, and when the said temperance man is ill—as is
frequently the case—the white of his eye is turned
gratefully to his medical man who suggests that he
requires a stimulant. More sentiment and Self-
deception! The self-made fence of fear about foods
and drinks would be laughable, were it not for its
serious side of mental demoralisation, self-deception,
mendacity, with ill-health of body. There is always
more or less of that induced and maintained by wrong
thinking—Auto-suggestions of fear and fancy.

There are many, as I have already said, cannot get
enough to eat. These are less than those who eat too
much, ay, and drink unwisely. There are many who
are perforce vegetarians perhaps as much from the

habits of their country-side and from poverty. But the poor and one-sided nourishment does not make either for physical powers or for mental stamina. When the St Gothard Tunnel was made, the Lombardy Italians— who were vegetarians—were incapable of doing the work on the one end of the Tunnel, which the Swiss, who used a moderate supply of meat in their dietary, were able to accomplish at the other. A greater variety of fruit and vegetables might with advantage form the bulk of food partaken, but to exclude fish, flesh, and fowl from our dietary would be a great mistake. *It is not so much the food itself which disagrees with the chronic dyspeptic—it is eating in excess of his requirements.* Should you happen to be one of those mentally demoralised, self-deceived, and ill of body dyspeptics, pitying and bemoaning your fate, please read this last sentence over again and think about it. There are many causes of dyspepsia, but this is the main one— eating in excess of your requirements. Less Self-pity and more Self-control is the Remedy. I knew a dyspeptic who would eat a pound of steak and a variety of other things at a meal, and only one potato. He blamed the potato.

In the matter of foods and drinks I am not a faddist, and no hard and fast lines can be laid down. So much depends on the individual, climate, employment, state of health, and what not. Man can live on flesh foods, or he can live just as well without. He has in all ages taken stimulants. He has generally erred in over-eating. Civilised or barbarian, his highest sense of enjoyment is a "good tuck-in." And he has not always been content with that. The man who means to succeed in life is never over-anxious about what he eats or drinks, but he controls his appetite and applies Moderation to all that he does. He does not force or tickle his appetite with sweets, wines, nuts, and fruits after he has already had sufficient food. He does not wash down plateful after plateful with liquids, or, worse still, alcoholised liquors. HE FINDS IT IS REALLY LESS IMPORTANT WHAT HE EATS, THAN WHEN. He calls nothing unclean which God has made for food. He discriminates, and of that which is good and useful he partakes in moderation, and that which is unserviceable HE ABSTAINS FROM. St Paul advised certain converts to " eat what is set before you and ask no questions." If this was a wise thing to do for conscience' sake, it would be a most sensible thing for most persons to do for their stomach's sake. In one's own home, we can or should be able to have a say in the quality and the particular kind of food, etc., which we prefer to partake, but in the house of a friend or as a guest we should eat cheerfully what is set before us—keeping the Law of Moderation before us. Your faddist, who parades his " Simple Life," and who cannot take this and won't take that and dare not eat the other thing, may be a good man, but has a most indelicate and nasty way of showing it. As a host, however, bear cheerfully with his " Simple Life," set him a good example, and enjoy what is set before you. Be a reformer if you like. Be a gentleman too.

With regard to drinking, a few lines will suffice. We can abstain from food when we cannot do without drink. We take a good deal of liquid in our foods, and, while this is helpful, it is not sufficient. Man needs a plentiful supply of good, clear water. Water and milk are man's most natural and useful drinks. Light cocoa, newly infused tea, and even now and then a cup of good, decent coffee can be used to advantage. The woman who desires beauty and the man who loves strength—which in both cases means health—will only use these preparations when properly made, and with great moderation. All liquids are best used sipped after a meal, or during a meal, when the mouth is empty of anything else. The best possible time for drinking freely is immediately on rising, between meals, and on retiring.

Among the many reasons given by some authorities for the increase of diseases, and the concomitant evils connected therewith, in the winter time, the inadequate use of liquids is one. Some recommend four quarts daily, but this seems to me to be absurd, and the foolish fad likely to create a hydro-anæmic condition of the blood, a proceeding as undesirable as anæmia induced by the folly of under-feeding, and living on unsuitable diets, such as strong tea, sweets, pickles, and white bread, so frequently indulged in by some of the future mothers of the British race.

It is, however, clear that the majority of persons do not drink enough in the winter time, and the blood suffers in consequence. Then the use of pure water is much neglected, and the usual practice is to take coffee, cocoa, or tea at breakfast, beer or some other alcoholised drink, with or without soda, at lunch or dinner—with possibly more drink of the same character at intervals during the day,—more tea at tea-time, and more beer or spirits, with or without coffee, at supper-time. Then again, ladies are devoted to tea, tea, tea, and sometimes a gentle stimulant of stronger character, but use little or no pure water—cold, filtered, or boiled—as an article for daily use. It need scarcely be suggested that these ill-advised methods or habits of drinking are not conducive to good health.

The excessive use of alcoholic liquids and other enervating drinks is decidedly disease-producing. I might add, a man in a *state of health* does not require alcoholic drinks, but is not likely to be injured by occasionally partaking of the same with food. In ill-health the use of alcohol is a doubtful expedient. Each case must be dealt with on its merits. A sensible man does not drink spirituous liquids in health, for that is unnecessary, and in ill-health will abstain therefrom, as a safe thing to do. The man who " drinks," because he does not like to say " No," is either a fool or a liar. He is generally both. It may be safely said, " The abstainer has the best of it." Little, indeed, can be said here in favour of the use of alcohol either in health or disease—and its misuse is beyond the scope of these pages. Teetotalism is not my theme, but Self-reliance—including Self-control—is. Apart from the dangers to oneself, the habitual use of alcohol is a *fertile* predisposing cause of mortality in infants, and tuberculosis—*the white plague*—and other phases of phthisis in those who have lived beyond the age of puberty. Alcohol, while it temporarily stimulates, also depraves and depresses the disease-resistance of the body, and should be abstained from as a beverage by all.

Water, milk and water, and the homely article, good butter-milk, should be employed more fully daily as blood-cleansers, also as an aid to all the secretions, so that there may be an adequate flow of saliva, gastric and pancreatic juice, and bile; likewise to promote gentle perspiration, and other processes of elimination. Constipation—that corrupter of the blood and vile product of over-eating and nerve starvation—is unknown where a liberal supply of good clean water and its equivalents is taken daily. All should use internally plenty of water to maintain health. As restoratives of health, the processes of water cure—from the enema to the compress and the hot-air bath—can be wisely employed in each household. The use of hot water—both internally, as a drink, and externally, in compresses, etc.—is an invaluable remedial agent. Internally, the frequent drinking of pure soft water, freshly boiled, is a good remedy for irritation and inflammation of œsophagus, stomach, and all internal organs. Mild lemonade, home made from lemons—not chemicals,— also from limes, grapes, oranges and similar fruit juices, will be found, in the words of a certain well-known advertisement of cocoa, "grateful and comforting."

Although it is not my intention now to deal with the treatment of diseases by hydropathy or other hygienic process, it will not be out of place here to emphasise the fact that the bulk of the victims of modern civilisation do not make a practice of drinking daily enough simple, pure liquids, of which clean, soft water is the most important. The abstinence from habits which are injurious, and the doing of those things which should be done, are all useful modes of improving the health and educating the Will at one and the same time. Value health, treasure it, and, if drinking more freely helps to lay down a good physical foundation for it, lay that foundation.

The question of "no breakfast" or "no supper," and the suitability of certain foods and drinks, and quantities—that can only be answered on its merits, having due regard to the individual and the circumstances. But when you are in doubt, there is SAFETY IN MODERATION.

To over-eating, constipation, and want of physical exercise, and to over-sleeping arising out of these indulgences, may be attributed the greater proportion of not only the diseases from which men suffer, but also of the failures in life.

I have now outlined what I mean by stomach rest. The benefits are enormous and the expense is nil. In innumerable cases it has been proved that, by reducing the ordinary supply of food to one-half and eating that properly, there has been a greater increase of vitality, energy, physical force, and mental power. For SUCCESS and usefulness in life, STOMACH REST is as essential as BRAIN REST.   As a closing note, when tired REST. Don't whine, be irritable, or waste time by retailing your feelings.   Just REST, and be sensible.

Possibly you have fallen into some errors in eating and drinking, and you have not exercised the care which you should have done.   Well, commence now to do what is right.

CULTIVATE THE VIGOUR OF ORGANISATION NECESSARY FOR TONE OF MIND.

WORK, WHEN WORK IS TO BE DONE.   DO IT CHEER-FULLY.

REST, WHEN REST IS NECESSARY.   DO IT THOROUGHLY.

DO NOT FORGET THAT BRAIN REST AND STOMACH REST ARE THE MOST IMPORTANT FOR SUCCESS.

LAY A GOOD FOUNDATION IN PHYSICAL HEALTH.

The preceding exercises will, both directly and indirectly, cultivate the WILL and improve the HEALTH and make for SUCCESS.

CHAPTER XI

" We have no light promised us to show us our road a hundred miles away, but we have light for the next footstep, and if we take that we shall have a light for the one which is to follow."— MARK RUTHERFORD.

YOU have in the preceding lessons received a few suggestions which, faithfully carried out in practice, will have done much to make a marked improvement in you. In order, however, to get greater benefits, so that, in addition to being able to hold your head erect, plant your feet firmly on the ground, control your impulses—your tongue—and master difficulties as they arise, you will now take another step in the right direction. That step is to sit still and take stock, as it were, and ascertain what your progress has been, so far, and what are your greatest defects. This done, face them clearly and squarely, and then set to work and MASTER THEM.

Ponder well over the qualities which you realise—through past experiences—you possess, and get to work to make more of them. It is old advice, and the best— do not put your light under a bushel. For your own sake as well as that of others, whatever you can do best,

that do. Strength comes in the using, joy and satisfaction in all well-meant attempts. Success is the
outcome of continued effort. There is growth and
progress through effort—none otherwise.

To encourage you, I take a few cases from my note-
book of some who were failures in their own estimation,
and would have continued to be, had they not learned
to take COURAGE and MASTERED their defects.

Leaving out those who have been the victims of
overwhelming evil habit, and taking ordinary representative cases, such as the man who feels he is
badly used, and always taken advantage of, and would
succeed in life if he had " Influence"—he is always a
noted failure.

It is admitted that success depends on merit or
fitness and on—in some cases—influence. This individual is a failure owing to the initial error of trust-
ing to others and not to himself, for success. Influence
is an important factor in success. But given merit,
character, or fitness—influence, like success, can always
be attracted in time and made good use of. Our
friend has been sitting down expecting the world
to come to him and recognise his great ability and
plead for his services, before having shown that his
services are worth asking for. This person was a
failure before he recognised the causes. When he
pulled himself together—became improved in physical
health, clearer in head, and sounder in mind—he was
able to work with a will and do what he had to do
well. Then he learned not only what success and

happiness were, but that "Influence" was there to back him up too.

There is another type, one who assures you, "I have no will; if I were like So-and-so, I'd be a very successful person. He seems to stick at nothing. He gets what he wants. He is so determined, and nothing daunts him. I am so sensitive, I could not do as he does." The man of the aforesaid type does not succeed for several reasons—the main reason being that he pities and then flatters himself. He consoles and assures himself—that he has no will. Flatters himself that he is so sensitive—possessing a refinement which the successful man has not, and so on. By this process of false reasoning hypnotises himself into the belief that his defects are a cloak of charity to cover up his sins of laziness and self-gratification—for which he has ever a ready excuse.

The man whom he credits with success because of his want of sensitiveness, plus determination, industry, and will-power, will in all probability be a successful man. Not perhaps successful in everything, but he has the gumption to cover up his defeats or failures, and does not go about wasting his own time and that of other people proclaiming them. He is known as a Trojan for work. He has a reputation for doing his best and scamping nothing. His reputation brings him influence, more work, and success. He trusts in himself. Others soon learn to trust in him, not so much for what he says he will do, as what his labours have accomplished.

I will take a few more cases, and then, perhaps, the next step you are to take will be all the clearer to you. One writer says: " I have charge over five hundred men and have to see a large amount of contract work done—as directed by my superiors. I do things at times with unconquerable firmness. At other times the merest trifle alters my mind. For instance, I have a friend who has great firmness; he is a vegetarian and goes in for the ' simple life,' and he is a successful man, in a way. If he sits at a table spread with the most tempting viands, etc., he will adhere to his plain food and water. I have often determined to do the same, but when I sit before a good table all my resolutions take flight. Again, I will spend hours working out a plan, solving all the difficulties, and see my way to do certain work or some new contract better than at first contemplated. I submit my plans to someone else for approval. Suggestions are made for alteration, or perhaps the plans are pooh-poohed, and I am influenced for the time and put them aside. Later on I discover that my plans have been the best. What I want is firmness to carry out what I have decided on. Instead of that, I am a creature of circumstances, and fail where I should succeed. "

The writer of the foregoing has my fullest sympathy. We recognise that there is no progress unless we change our minds. Unfortunately, he changes his at the wrong time. Here we have industry and also capacity, as evidenced in his responsible position. He can carry out the orders of his superiors; what he lacks is *a knowledge of his own mental powers.* As for his friend, it may be comparatively easy for him to abstain from the " wine when it is red," and the " flesh-pots of Egypt " to boot, not because he has more firm-ness, but because his appetite for these things is not either by inheritance or indulgence built that way. It is well to know oneself. This letter-writer has what phrenologists call " large alimentiveness," and, with a vigorous and somewhat vital organisation, takes pleasure in eating, and perhaps in drinking. He has also " large approbativeness," and is fond of praise, and is therefore easily disconcerted by censure ; moderate in " secretive-ness," and hence his seeking approval, and talking about " What I was thinking would be a good thing " to others, before he carries out the good thing into practice. He does not know that the faculties or the propensities which are most prominent in his mental constitution are those which most readily seek their gratification. He does not lack WILL-power so much as a knowledge of himself. Learning his own defects, this contractor's right-hand man soon learned to manage himself, as he had from experience and necessity learned to manage the varied workmen under his control. He discovers that he has firmness—A WILL. Also that there is no royal road by which mastery can be obtained without plodding, persistent, and renewed endeavour. Putting into practice my suggestions, he succeeds eventually where much before had been comparative failure.

The man who realises what his failures are, and is

fully convinced of the necessity to remedy them, conjoined with the sincere desire to overcome them, has
indeed that kind of intelligence which makes for
success eventually.

In the following case, that of an intelligent man
feeling his difficulties, we have an illustration of the
fact that they mainly arise from his lack of knowledge
of himself.   He is in India, that land of the " Handicap
of Life," with few white confrères and abundant trials
in his environment.   He writes :—" Will you help me ?
I am prompted to write to you after reading your book,
The Practical Hypnotist.   I am thirty years of age, and
for the last fifteen years have been deeply interested in
psychical subjects. . . . I have read many works on
Hypnotism . . . and I earnestly desire to know more
of what are termed psychic phenomena.   Before this,
however, can be, I must first control myself.   It is for
this I seek your help.   Physically, I am slightly built,
fairly healthy, not robust though.   I am a lifelong
teetotaler, moderate smoker.   Morally, I live a clean
life.   Although I have will-power to a certain extent,
I am obstinate—I have no real will ; no perseverance.
If I decide to take a certain course, I do so vigorously
for a few days, and then imperceptibly I begin to
slacken, until at last I realise with some surprise that
I have ceased to do whatever it may have been.   I
have said I have no will, but perhaps inability to concentrate my mind is the great weakness.   *I desire that
gift of being able to set myself in a way and to pursue it
to the end.*"   The italics are mine.

This client has a highly nervous, active, impression-able organisation; plenty of spirit, but not much physical staying power; and being bright and sanguine, he takes a sudden interest in some pursuit or study, starts off by *attempting too much*—unduly taxing his mental faculties in one special direction—and with the dulling of the brain-centres employed gradually loses interest. Other portions of his brain being more active, he either switches off on new lines, or, what is more likely, into his old habits again.

This is a case where, attempting less, he would accomplish more. It is a good thing to learn how to do "one thing at a time," and not attempt too much. Only be thorough while at it. In this case the evident mental defect was want of real interest to produce the requisite concentration. He has given hours to a new study for a few days, and then wearied in well-doing. What is wanted is a real conviction to start with, that such and such a course is necessary, that it is the one for which he is best adapted. Having settled these points in the affirmative, the next step is to do a small but systematic amount of study each day, and the end will soon be gained. He is a "new chum," and by the time he has put in his paces, he will be able to overcome his want of concentration.

I know a very busy physician, who is medical adviser to a large hydropathic establishment and the medical officer of health for an important sea-coast burgh, and also possesses a large private general practice. In four short months he mastered Esperanto, and delivered a

most interesting lecture on the subject. How did he
manage that? By utilising the few spare moments he
had while waiting for meals, and in his carriage when
going from patient to patient. Where willing, none are
too old to learn, and find time to study. Mr Gladstone
commenced the study of Greek at seventy-two : William
Blake was sixty-seven when he commenced to study
Italian : Arkwright the inventor was fifty years of age
before he began to study mysteries of grammar and
spelling : the late Queen Victoria was over seventy
when she commenced the study of Hindustani, that
she might converse with some of her Indian subjects.
And I know one busy man, who learned typewriting
at fifty-six, and shorthand two years later, to facilitate
his professional work.

You will find that the busy man—the genuine article
—can always find time to do more. It is to be noted
that, the less one has to do, the more easy it is to find
excuses to do less. You will have sufficient knowledge
of yourself and of human nature generally, to know
the foregoing to be true, and will be wise enough to
take a hint therefrom.

The next thing to be considered is the spirit in
which a man goes to work. Without the right spirit,
industry and proper application—which make for
success—are well-nigh impossible. Men fail frequently
because—although in a passable situation in which or
from its nature there is no prospect of advancement—
they do not work in the right spirit. They become
pessimistic, slovenly, and careless. Although there be

no prospect of advancement in the present post, they should do their work well where they are, and in their spare time, both within and after hours, *fit* themselves for something better.   The dispirited one not only does his work in a very perfunctory way, but he loses sight of the fact that work well done in a low grade will help to fit him for better work when it comes his way, or when he seeks it.   Again, many a man who wastes his time with amiable nothings and amusements, if nothing worse, "after hours," *fails, when the lad who improves himself " after hours " succeeds.*

In science no fact—however apparently trivial to most of us—is insignificant.   The falling of an apple arrested the attention of Newton, and led to the discovery of gravitation and its laws.   The bobbing of the lid of a kettle led Watt to the discovery of the motor force of steam.   The boy's kite, in the hands of Franklin, brought the world of science in touch with electricity, and the lightning conductor soon became a necessity and a safe commercial investment.   Other instances might be given.   You may not be a Newton, a Watt, or a Franklin, but you are one of those who wish to lay a foundation for success.   If you do, pay attention to little things—improvements, savings, inventions—and among the savings, the saving of time.   By a little order and method you will do well and gain by that.   The doctor mentioned learned Esperanto by utilising spare moments; you may learn shorthand, by giving fifteen to twenty minutes a day to it, which will have a commercial value in less than six months.   If a clerk in an office, you may pick up typewriting, in having ten minutes' to twenty minutes' practice at a machine during the lunch hour, when the typist is not on duty. You can learn a modern language—French, German—which will be more valuable to you than either short-hand or typewriting in a commercial sense—in, say, six months, by half an hour's study a day. Take one, or perhaps not more than two subjects at a time. Little by little, step by step, makes for success. Do you want to improve your memory? Note the points in which you are most defective: a few odd moments daily given to the subject—history, geography, weights, measures, money, etc.—will in a few months bring its reward. In those few odd moments you will be concentrating your attention in a special way, to a special end, and at the same time you will be cultivating Will indirectly—Self-reliance. Value small things: pence, small savings; make investments such as have laid the foundations for many a fortune; but above all small things, remember the odd moments which *cost you nothing*, and, rightly employed, will help you to build up that character and ability for which there is a constant demand with appropriate rewards in all spheres of life.

Do not consider the work which you are now doing beneath you—except in the sense of making a stepping-stone of it to something better. The order, taste, application which you now employ, the intelligence and the skill which you now use, will be of value when you come to attack greater responsibilities. Who knows but that, waking up out of your little defects, you may become a VITALISER in your own business, and convert it into something worthy of the name? On a low grade, a poor job is always better than none; a man in a situation is more likely to get something better than the man "with ideas" who loafs about, waiting for something to turn up. It is not the man who does what he likes, but the man who likes what he has to do, succeeds. Take an interest in what you are at, and you will soon be able to get a larger and wider sphere of usefulness.

There is a great deal in the spirit in which one approaches and carries out whatever he has in hand. There are more ways than one of illustrating " Where there is a will there is a way."

It is related of the late Lord Napier that once he played a trick on some young officers to find out the right man for a certain post. The story is that he had three ambitious officers to choose from, all of whom would like to be colonels at once. Lord Napier sent for these young men, and in due order detailed them to some ordinary routine work to be done. They went to their work without suspecting that the General wished to test them, and was having them watched for that purpose. The first two, whom I will call " A " and " B," considered the duties very much beneath them, and discharged them in a very careless and perfunctory manner, while complaining of the affront which they had received in being asked to discharge those duties. The third young officer was very prompt,.energetic, and thorough, and acquitted himself with credit.

" How is it," demanded Lord Napier, " that you thought such matters worthy of so much care ? " The young fellow flushed. He thought the General believed that he was an officer who had wasted too much energy on matters of no great moment.

" Beg pardon, General," he answered, " but it was just the fun of seeing how well I could do them."

The grim old General's face relaxed into a pleasant smile, and he said : " You are promoted to a captaincy. Go and see how much fun you can get in doing your best in that position."

I do not think that I need point out the moral of this little story. Promotion came here without " purchasing the next step." Influence came without crying for it. The spirit in which the work was done brought the success and the influence too. Do you your little bit right, and influence will in time back you up. It is the spirit which a man puts into his work which makes for success. You will not succeed in that in which you are not interested, and, indeed, not even in that which is better, without an effort—honest, continuous effort. The quickest and best way to make headway, is to do what lies nearest at hand in a way which will prove that you are fit for better work. It is not by being smart and flippant, by envying the man across the street or the man above you, that you will help yourself. It is not by wasting your temper and souring your spirit you will achieve success. It is the resolute, cheerful spirit, *guided by intelligence and a determined aim* to succeed, which creates SUCCESS.

To succeed, you require to study yourself, thoroughly get at your defects, and also make sure of that for which you are best adapted. You are not likely to concentrate your mind on pursuits for which you are not adapted, but you can on many things which you are qualified to accomplish. Everything lies in yourself primarily, not in others, in environment or in influence. The key of the situation lies in WHAT YOU DO and HOW YOU DO IT.

Concentration, like memory, is not an elementary faculty of the mind, but a function of the whole intellectual faculties. Some of these may be more powerful than others. For instance, you may have a keener ear for melody than others, or you may have better sense of time, calculation, order, memory for events, or possibly reasoning powers; hence your ability to concentrate your mind more effectually in one direction than in another. Well, consider in what other direction that power of concentration is weak. Then dwell on the necessity of improvement in that particular. If there be no real necessity, waste no time over it, but make the best use of those other powers you have. To do this there must be a *moral purpose*—a real aim—not a fanciful desire to accomplish something that someone else has done. It is good to imitate that which is best in others, as long as you do not neglect whatever is best in yourself.

While it is true that what one man has done another can do, it is nearer the truth to say, as it is truer in practice, that there is always something which one can do better than another. I am able to do things which you would not do as well, and you can do things successfully in which I would make a very poor show. The same suit will not fit everybody. The same cloth might do, but the cut and the dimensions must be different to fit; but even this won't do. You are not a tailor's block. You must have individuality in yourself and in your clothes too. Do you follow me? BE YOURSELF. Strike out in that for which your head, heart, and conscience intimate you are best fitted. Strike out; don't dream, much less talk about it. Set yourself to work and do it. It is like getting out of bed in the morning; *just rise*, the rest will come all right.

It is well not only to *go in* for that for which you are best fitted, but to bring freshness into it. Without this, that which is done will lack vitality, go, thoroughness. You cannot bring freshness into your work without laying down a good foundation of physical health. I have in former lessons pointed out some methods of securing it. To succeed, do not attempt to do twenty-four hours' work in a working day of ten or twelve. Curtail your work and your hours when that can be done, but bring freshness into all which has to be done. The freshness required comes from "high ideals," the right tone of thought, no doubt; but while we are in the flesh, it is best to get as much as possible out of sound sleep, moderate and nourishing meals, deep breathing, and a reasonable or a fair amount of attention to ordinary hygiene. One client writes, he feels that the time given to the breathing exercises is a waste of time.

And yet his failures in health and in business have almost wholly arisen from impatience. That is not the way freshness is to be obtained. Better stick to the breathing exercises. Give them a fair trial, and see what will truly come from learning the A B C of self-control. It will prove more profitable than impatience, and it is fresher and sweeter too. Stupid living, hasty meals, improper food, lack of sufficient sleep, late hours, dissipation, etc., are incompatible with freshness for work—and success.

The morning is the best time for attacking the serious work of the day, and hence one's best energies and time should be devoted to work then. Business first and pleasure afterwards, should be the rule. Whatever you are doing—whether writing a letter, doing mere routine work, directing and laying out work for others—be spry, fresh, energetic in doing that, and infuse life and go into your subordinates. You will feel all the better for it, and they will be affected by your influence and do your work all the better.

BE BRIGHT, BE FRESH, BE WILLING, and adopt the best means of being all this, and in that way PERSONAL MAGNETISM AND SUCCESS ARE YOURS.

Keep well: I have shown you how—so far. If you are not up to the mark, that will show itself in your work. To keep well, do not attempt too much, neither be lazy; you won't be either when you come to your work fresh. Make it your business to do so. Where your interest lies, there will your concentration be.

To keep well, again let me say, do not attempt too much, but keep at it. It is the continued effort in the right direction which tells. Give yourself a chance. Stop flurry, watch impatience, anger, excitement, and rise above all these unmanly trifles. Avoid worry. It is a bad hole to get into, and there is much good energy wasted in getting out. Let there be no such word in your lexicon as FEAR. Fear and depression belong to sluggish livers and poorly nourished brains. Keep well. Keep a clean body ; remember the hints on eating. Don't be afraid of wasting time by giving a few minutes daily to deep breathing. Don't be afraid of fresh air, and don't forget that all these blessings are to be had for the having, and are as cheap as a healthy, pleasant smile, and that an urbane manner, although the characteristic of the gentleman, costs nothing,—is a valuable asset in business and without price in the domestic circle.

I have noticed that many capable men have failed in life in consequence of periods of inaction, perhaps of several days or weeks of non-employment. They become indifferent, shifty, and where they do not actually reach the depths of the unemployable, they help to swell the ranks of the unemployed—not always in the sense of that term,—and they nevertheless become, under various plausible excuses, hangers, if not spongers, on the good-nature, grace, and patience of their relatives. I need not point a moral here. Keep at it. Every day a bit; no day without a line—something accomplished. That is the way to keep FIT as

well as WELL.   Give way to indifference, to laziness, to
weariness and retiring at unreasonable hours, and
hugging the blankets in the morning when you should
be up, and you are a ruined man.

Take yourself firmly in hand—or in both hands, if
necessary,—put out a little effort, and it will soon be
found that all feared troubles as well as self-created
ones will leave you.   As you determine, so you will be.
As Browning says, "It is the lifted face that feels the
shining of the sun."   The Infinite has given you the
sun, and the power, but it is yours to do the lifting of
the face.

CHAPTER XII

THE POWER AND DIGNITY OF LABOUR

"It may be proved with much certainty that God intends no man to live in this world without working ; but it seems no less evident that He intends every man to be happy in his work. It was written, 'In the sweat of thy brow,' but it was never written, 'In the breaking of thy heart.'"—RUSKIN.

IN the last lesson I called your attention to some stepping-stones to Will-power and Success, such as :— the necessity of effort ; the value of influence, and how to secure it ; some misconceptions about the Will, and various methods of improvement ; the study of your own powers, your gifts and defects ; and the spirit of work by which to attack all difficulties in order to succeed. In this we will consider together two or three more features of interest, and if you after careful reading and thoughtful consideration approve, carry out whatever is best into practice.

Read what is written with a purpose. Let that purpose be not so much to criticise the way in which the information is given, as the best way to gain some practical benefit from it. This is one of the best ways to do all your reading. A man may be a great reader and yet a fool—without one pennyworth of originality or grit in his composition : often as not a waster of valuable time, and a sufferer from chronic mental indigestion, which almost always mean the possession of a "poor memory" and an unstable disposition. When you read, take time, and now and then weigh the advice given ; under-score and even memorise whatever you esteem most useful. Do not hurry. Ask yourself—if need be—Do I understand ? Shall I be any wiser or better for carrying out the hints given ? Am I neglecting other and more important duties while reading ? If satisfied that you are not, then read slowly and thoughtfully, and you will truly grasp the end for which they are written ; and, better still, get more fully into harmony with the spirit of the writer, and be thus aroused and encouraged in the battle for victory which you have set yourself on gaining.

Let the same method of reading be adapted for general self-culture. Select a few of the best books; read them in the above manner. Where possible, re-read, as would a lover of Shakespeare, Byron, Burns, or Scott, the books of your favourite authors. For special training or culture, select such works—not many, a few and good—as are most suited for your work, profession, etc. ; and peruse them carefully, a little at a time. Take that well in, before going further. In this way you will read with profit, and have a well-stored mind, getting many fresh aids to thought and work. The hasty reading of matter indiscriminately selected is not only a waste of time, but it is subversive of all right thinking. Without right thinking there will be no success.

Labour has been esteemed a curse by the shallow-minded. The love of idleness is a characteristic of the unenlightened, the brand of aristocracy; while labour is delegated to inferiors as something mean and unworthy. Some of us have been taught that labour is a curse and a punishment entailed on man—according to the picturesque language of the Hebrew Scriptures—owing to the sin of our first parents. If so, THE PUNISHMENTS OF GOD ARE BLESSINGS. Although man may have to earn his bread by the sweat of his brow, labour is a blessing of the very highest character. If at times that blessing is disguised from our vision by our mental fogs and dislikes, it is a blessing in the truest sense. To despise labour or work is a sign of an unhealthy and ill-disciplined mind. It is true that, owing to unequal social conditions, as the outcome of the ignorance as well as differences in capacity of the various units of mankind, some are unduly exploited by their more astute fellows ; but this does not alter the truth that labour is a blessing. As these lessons are not a treatise on social and political economy, the foregoing must suffice. My object is to assist you in your individual progress. Let the foolish despise work; as for you, learn to honour and appreciate it. Labour will not degrade you. See to it that you do not degrade your work by misapplication, indifference, or worse.

" No one is so maimed or imprisoned but God has

a bit of work for him to do somewhere." It is one of the encouraging marvels of life, how the delicate, crippled, blind, deaf, dumb, and otherwise maimed have succeeded in bearing life's burdens. Notwithstanding limitations of mental sense and body, they have been able to work, and rejoice that they have been able to do so. They have been able—in their own special sphere—to support themselves, while their cheerfulness and industry have been truly object-lessons to others. But these lessons are not for the lame, the halt, and the blind, but for you—you who are normally endowed—so that you may, by the hints which they contain, make the best possible use of the powers which you now possess, and increase both them and your opportunities by labour.

The unemployed (whether of choice, as—with some —in the upper ranks of society, or in any class who will do anything rather than work; or from necessity—in the lower—as sometimes happens) are mostly degenerates—the centre and the source of the vicious, the criminal, the submerged, and the helpless. Without employing and utilising our powers in labour—self-culture—suitable to our physical and mental endowments, we deteriorate in both mind and body.

From your acquaintance with your fellow-men, and from a little reflection on the tendencies of your own nature, in conjunction with your own actual experience in the past, you will learn to realise that the following statements are true :—

(a) Labour is a necessity as well as a blessing.

(*b*) Labour develops your Self-reliance, *i.e.* your mental powers, and enhances your physical energies, contributing by the exercise of your faculties—in proper and orderly methods—to your well-being and unfoldment.

(*c*) The more competent you are to labour—according to your fitness and the sphere in which you move—the more value you are as a man, and the more important your position. Consequently labour is a blessing to be coveted and prized, not only by yourself, but by all who are dependent on your initiative, industry, and sterling worth.

(*d*) Labour is the most laudable and healthy means by which you earn your daily bread. Give that word " bread " the widest significance.

You are justly entitled to accept as a bit of sound philosophy, that every man who comes into the world is an inheritor of all that is good in himself and in the world. He is entitled to a living at least—to a healthy, sane, well-nourished state of being—but unless he is prepared to work for that living by the exercise of his faculties, in some capacity according to fitness, he will fail to get that living—his faculties will fail to reach development, and as a result he will be numbered among the failures in life.

HEALTH, WEALTH, AND SUCCESS are prizes to be obtained as the fruits of labour, in the broadest and truest sense of that term. Labour is the salt of the earth, and all that which is worth having can be obtained by working for it. You succeed in life by individual effort—by what you do. If all that is good, pure, healthful, noble, and useful, all that makes life worth having and living, is to be obtained as the fruits of labour, why not only work for these, but in every reasonable way prepare yourself for the task? If you admire good qualities in others; are pleased with their qualities of mind, patience, perseverance, energy, application, fortitude, sweetness of disposition; if you are enthused and invigorated by contact and proximity of such examples, let them be an inspiration to you. And aim to be in your sphere, as they are in theirs, worthy of all that is best in you. Every effort you make in the right direction increases your power for good.

In addition to the suggestions already given, I will venture another, and that is, throw yourself into your ideals in a whole-hearted way, with faith, thoroughness, and energy; and in seeking to realise them, *get away from self* as much as possible. Many of my correspondents have failed in life through self-consciousness or that nervous fear of others, or at least that form of it which dreads what others may or may not think. If you are troubled with this sort of self-consciousness, *get rid of it.*

Fear of any kind is bad, but this kind of egotistical fear, which is eternally in operation about oneself, is the silliest and most contemptible of all hindrances. It is a permissible weakness in a school miss, and we simply smile and pass on when we see her concerned about her looks, her poses, and how this and that other

speech or action of hers will be taken, with her ever-
lasting "I," of half-asserted confidences. But in the
man of sense and self-government, self-consciousness,
timidity, and fears for self have no place. This self-
consciousness is distinctly effeminate. It is a fondness
of self, and a pitying of self which is as senseless as it
is contemptible. Let me urge you to believe in yourself,
in all that is good and strong in yourself. Do what
you esteem to be right, and let no self-consciousness
hinder you in the doing of that.

I admit that some great men—that is, men who have
by their successful labours achieved distinction—are
egotists, and have their periods of self-consciousness.
But it is never of that effeminate kind which hinders
them in their work. After work well done comes the
period of praise from their fellows and laudable self-
satisfaction to themselves. This is self-consciousness
of the right kind. It is both human and desirable to
be fond of praise. Let it be earned, and by all means
deserved. Whether obtained or not, it should be no
hindrance to one's labours. That which is most to be
valued will be found in the work itself. The true
artist *forgets* himself in his work; the workman works
best when his mind is absorbed by what he is doing;
even so your moments of vision, of clear-mindedness,
will come when you get rid of and are lifted above self.
The highest efficiency is gained when you become
forgetful of self, and are not hindered by the *fear of
a fear about yourself*, of your appearance, of your
ability, your manner, your work, or about the censure

or the appreciation of either your friends or of the world—when you put your best into the task in hand, regardless of these things. Don't say, "I fail to do this," or "I cannot do that," until you have really tested yourself. On a lower but still necessary plane, the less self-consciousness a man has the better. There would be less ill-health, less feeling and dreading of this or that emotion or pain, if the mind was interested or absorbed in the duties or, for that matter, in the relaxations of life.

Self-consciousness is and has ever been a hindrance to success. Some persons are happy, and unconscious in ordinary circumstances of this weakness, but the moment they enter upon new conditions they become troubled, harassed, and fearful about themselves, and may therefore, and for that reason, suffer disadvantage. The speaker trembles before a new audience, or the actor has something of stage fright; the applicant for a new position feels backward and so forth, and is confused when addressed. All the self-consciousness leaves as the speaker enters into his theme, the actor into his part, the applicant into his work. *The more genuineness, sincerity, and determination there is in a man's composition, the less self-consciousness does he possess. He has no time, no thought, to waste on self, emotions, feelings, etc.*

What is true of the great is also true of the less notable, with this difference, that the latter are troubled with more self-consciousness than the former. Some have the sense to know it is a weakness, master it, and steadily achieve success.   There are many—far too many—who, in proportion to their non-success, make up for it in pointless egotism, and in incessant talking about their sensitiveness, delicacy, fears—real and imaginary—causes of failure, and finally and always about themselves.   It is not in this waste of energies that growth, progress, and success are to be cultured.

The best remedy for this self-consciousness is to be found :—

Firstly.—In self-discipline on the lines already indicated in these lessons, in which deep and correct breathing under the conscious control of the WILL forms a feature.   This, leading to the control of thought, giving pause to collect oneself in a sudden emergency, and materially aiding in one's self-culture, only needs to be thoroughly tried to prove its efficiency.

Secondly. — In simple Non-comatose suggestions, properly and systematically administered, dealing with this weakness or other defects of which you are conscious and desire to remedy.   The art and practice of Non-comatose Auto-suggestions will be explained in subsequent lessons.   Meanwhile a brief exercise is attached to this one.

Thirdly.—On all and every possible occasion, practise Self-reliance.   Be it.   Seek and be high-minded, honourable, self-confident, dignified, reserved, and courteous.   Esteem it the highest honour in life to be a man.   Live up to a worthy ideal of manhood.   Whatever your position, regard your work and your position seriously and thoroughly.   Do your work with the faithfulness and the honour you would expect and probably demand from a subordinate. Aim to stand at the head of your profession. Believe in yourself; accept and never shirk responsibilities. Cultivate the acquaintance of the most worthy, thorough, noble, and reliable man in your circle. Think more of yourself, and reflect your good sense and quiet dignity on your associates, so that your poorest servant will be helped thereby. By all means cultivate a good, reliable, and honest estimate of yourself—and live up to it.

Fourthly.—In going about the duties of life, either those imposed on you by your employment or selected by yourself, quietly adapt yourself with as little delay as possible to what is to be done or discharged. Whatever is to be done, do it cheerfully and thoroughly. Attack the work in the order in which it should be accomplished. If need be, do that which is most disagreeable or difficult first. Master that, and the rest will come easier, if not more as a form of relaxation. " After labour comes refreshment," according to ancient Masonic practice. To obtain the latter, get the former attended to.

You will find the foregoing methods of absorption in work a true cure for all self-consciousness; and your method of procedure presupposes that *either you are trained for your work or you are training yourself now.* And this forethought or preparation gives confidence, and in doing that for which you are best fitted all the elements which make for self-consciousness are minimised. This self-consciousness must be got rid of, and the foregoing methods are the simplest and the readiest by which you can and WILL ACHIEVE THE VICTORY. They will enhance your Will-power, Concentrativeness, Self-reliance, and give you Success, where all has been a comparative failure.

That which you are determined to do, and quietly and systematically continue to pursue, you will finally accomplish. Coarse natures are hindered by vices; the more refined by self-consciousness. The majority of failures can be traced to both vices and self-consciousness.

Just another thought, and that from Tolstoy:—". We forget that there may be many duties, but among them there is a first and a last, and that we must not fulfil the last before fulfilling the first, just as one must not harrow without ploughing."

Possibly you may feel that you are not troubled with self-consciousness so much as you are hindered by your surroundings. Possibly not. There are many who think that way. They blame their surroundings for failure in life. If only they had been somewhere else they would have done so much better. This is all idle talk, like to that of the woman who is sorry that she was not born a man; or that of the old man who would do " so and so," if only he had his life to live over again. That there is an influence in environment is admitted; but if you are wise you will never lose sight of the motive of these lessons—that the causes of success lie in oneself. If you would be successful, believe in and trust yourself. It is quite true that

men have succeeded abroad who might or might not
have done well at home.   We have numerous examples
of Irishmen and Scotchmen who have done well abroad.
They possibly had a larger field for their industry,
enterprise, and general abilities.   At home they may
have been limited—we do not know—in opportunities ;
hampered by obsolete ideas about position, about trade,
and possibly about conventionality.   Possibly at home
they did not like to do this thing or to do that, because
their family might not like it, although the thing
itself might be honest and honourable enough.   Or
they may have been brought up to certain professions
or trades, and they do not like to engage in any other
—while at home.   All these phases of self-consciousness
may have hindered their progress at home.   Abroad,
these hindrances appear to have vanished—with a
vengeance sometimes.   Those who learn to do whatever
is handiest, succeed and live—while others   starve.
House decorators are not wanted in Greenland, nor are
professors of skating required in Ceylon.   The "new
chum" must put his hand to the work nearest him—
if he has got the right stuff in him he will succeed.
He has got his opportunity and will make the best
of it, or die in the attempt.   That is the Spirit of
Success.

Many a clerk doing fairly good work at home, but
finding that he is somewhat poorly paid, decides to go
abroad.   He discovers, however, that his special talents
in writing and copying letters are not wanted.   If
willing to work and face the music, he becomes a

successful sheep farmer in one colony, or a planter, farmer, or trader in another. Success comes to the man willing to work. The ne'er-do-well at home is not the material which succeeds abroad, and our colonies, which offer many inducements, have no room for the man that is "born tired" or for that makeshift the "incessant grumbler." Where there is a will there is a way—at home as well as abroad. Wherever you may be, make the most of and take the most out of your circumstances. It is for you to conquer the circumstances. It is not the environment which makes the man, but his seizing and making the most of his environment. It is not work which has killed half as many as rust and the wasting of valuable energies unworthy of the true spirit of manhood—these have strewn the shores of the Empire at home and abroad with human wrecks. Some men who have *failed* at home, think by changing their name and going abroad they will do better. They may change both their name and country, but wherever they go they will take *themselves* with them, and unless they change their ways for the better, no mere change of environment will help them.

It is for you to find out what is best in you, and make the most of it. ALL IS YOURS IF YOU WILL TRULY HAVE IT SO. No workman's idle dreaming. You will get what you work for—and you are getting it now.

Many "New Thought" teachers have arisen of late years, at home and abroad, who emphasise the powers of the human mind; the ascendency and potentiality of thought; the efficiency of Affirmations—Non-comatose Suggestions—as the great secret by which Personal Magnetism, Will-power, and Success are to be obtained. But rest assured that while truth lies in that direction, it is not the whole truth. However great your natural endowments, however aspiring your thoughts and perfectly phrased your affirmations, unless these are consciously materialised by practice — practice, labour, or work—your thoughts and all the high-sounding talk about them are merely "words words, words." They are valueless; worse than valueless. Many imagine they have only to think fine thoughts, or repeat the thoughts of others; to desire this particular thing or that, and then "Affirm," in order to possess it, or "Deny" in order to get rid of something—pain, evil, or loss, which at times are very real to most of us. While claiming or affirming "I and God are one," "I am God," "I am all-powerful," "I am perfect," so seriously set forth by these transatlantic, transcendental "Scientists," can only be described as idle and mischievous nonsense, I believe in the power of thought, in the transcendent influence of the dominant mental attitude. I know something of the value of creating deliberately, CHEERFUL, POSITIVE, and OPTIMISTIC THOUGHTS, and of ignoring and discounting pain and loss—in thought. I also know these thoughts must be followed by action. We must DO as well as think. All that is worth having or likely to contribute to our well-being must be worked for, at our best, and according to our fitness and opportunities.

Granted that we equip or fit ourselves for and make or seize hold of opportunities, still the foregoing remains true—our mind powers, thoughts of the right sort, desires, ambitions, must be transmuted by labour into the gold of conscious possession.

You have not only to desire, to think, but to think in a definite way, on definite lines, and to bring your actions into line with your thoughts, with all your heart and soul—then you will enter into the joy of possession and the rewards of your labour.

The following brief exercise will be found of service in helping to discipline thought, in concentrating on a distinct line of thought, and in controlling and directing the powers of the body.

Lie with loosened clothes on the flat of your back— before rising and after retiring being most suitable times. Inhale slowly, deeply, and thoroughly, and hold the breath. While doing so tense all the muscles of the body gradually. Do what you can in the ten or fifteen seconds in which you are able to hold your breath. Commence with the hands and arms. Close the fist and tense the muscles of the latter. Then stretch out the toes and tense the muscles of the calf and the loins. In due time you will be able to contract and tense the muscles of the abdomen, chest, and back. Proceed gradually and be content to manage the arms and legs at first. When at fullest tensity your thoughts will be most positive. Let them be clear and brief, as, for instance: "I am healthy, happy, and cheerful." "I am resolute, strong, and decided." They will fulfil their mission when they by repetition and action become incorporated in Self.

When you have held the tension as long as you can —without cramp, strain, or undue distress—relax slowly and exhale gradually. Pause for a short time, say two or three seconds, while you fix your mind on the thoughts which you would mentally inspire. Then repeat the whole exercise slowly and cautiously, at least eight or ten times at each full exercise. At the conclusion take at least ten minutes' absolute rest— motionless rest.

Apart from the improvement in mental power, you will be conscious, while lying perfectly still, of various tingling sensations or vibrations in all the organs of the body. These indicate the addition of vital nerve force or magnetism, by which the whole brain and nervous system have been invigorated.

The exercise brings into play two qualities of mind and body. First, a quiet and receptive mood of mind, with relaxed muscles of the body. Second, a positive and executive state of mind, with firmness or tensity of muscle. The whole being under the control of the Will—the Intellect—tends to general improvement, with increasingly marked development of self-control. These exercises may take the place of previous ones; should be continued twice a day for a month or six weeks, and thereafter whenever you feel the need.

Now be of good courage. Do not let disappointments depress you, or want of immediate success harass you. Disappointments should be always taken as a stimulant and never viewed as a discouragement. For instance, I am fond of fishing. I do not always get fish when plying the rod, but rest assured I do get more fish than the man who does not try. Putting oneself in the way of success is evidently the best method of obtaining it.

CHAPTER XIII

CONCENTRATION, ORDER, AND PUNCTUALITY

"Do not act as if you had ten thousand years to throw away. Death stands at your elbow. Be good for something while you live and it is in your power."—MARCUS AURELIUS.

THE man whose aim in life "is to pass the time away" is a self-confessed failure. He neither appreciates the value of life nor respects himself. He is bartering away his inherited rights for a mess of immediate self-gratification. The majority of the failures in life are traceable to a lack of Self-reliance plus want of Concentration, Order, and to Procrastination. The Power of Continuity is necessary to success in all departments of life as well as in professional careers. An excess of Continuity, which is exhibited in prolixity and excessive amplification, absent-mindedness, and brooding over some one line of thought, is as undesirable as deficiency, which exhibits itself in excessive love of variety, impetuousness, lack of patience, the power of application and self-control.

The power of the mind to dwell on the preliminary steps to be taken, and then the promptitude and diligence in having them carried out in an orderly, systematic, and thorough fashion in every essential detail, certainly goes a long way in the direction of success. In fact, success is impossible without a good share of this industrial stick-to-it-tiveness.

With some temperaments there is a good deal of hustle and bustle in everything they do—more sail than ballast, in fact. In these days the hustling man passes for a man of thorough enterprise in business. There is nothing like activity, energy, and enterprise; but before hustling counts for anything in business or in any other calling, there must be not only experience, but there must be that training of self in which Concentration, Order, and Punctuality are developed. With these personal qualities, conjoined to business experience—training in one's work—energy, activity —hustling tells, not otherwise. Without the Self-reliance, personal self-control and discipline which steady application to duty develops, no amount of hustling will be of any service. Granted that a man has a fair grasp of his business, a knowledge of his public, then let him concentrate on the best means to discharge the first, that he may secure the fullest patronage of the latter. Without ability to do this, push, impatient energy, hustling, merely means disaster in business and mental breakdown to the individual. The hustler, in nine cases out of ten, does not take time to think, to count the cost, with the result that he has too many things in hand; one thing after another fails, because he could not devote the attention which the matter deserved. Possibly failure too, has arisen from shortage in capital, lack of time to mature the undertaking. All of which might have been avoided by looking forward a little, attempting less, and BY GIVING MORE THOROUGH ATTENTION TO THE WORK IN HAND. Had this been done, his energies would have been concentrated; there would have been more order and method; procrastination—meaning neglect of attention to some things —would have been avoided, and greater success for what he had in hand assured. Why? Because he had greater control over each undertaking, greater control over himself, and—at any rate—his chances of failure would be minimised by the forethought and the thoroughness which he was able to put into his business.

Concentration—sometimes called "Continuity"—is not possessed by all men alike. It is not expected that should be so. Some wish to qualify themselves for success in one special line of thought, business, or mechanics. Others desire to possess a nodding acquaintance with a variety of pursuits and a general knowledge of things, and seem to do pretty well with this outlook. A good deal, however, of the power of concentrated thought is required in scientific, scholastic, philosophic, legal pursuits; and in all large undertakings where it is important, several branches have to be carried out, and special studies, inquiries, and applications attended to. In these cases where there is the superintending head or principal, there must be devolution in work, every department having its responsible manager. The business or undertaking becomes successful from the organising capacity of the principal and the faithful services of those carrying out his orders. In smaller concerns failure comes from attempting too much—one man attempting to do the work of two or three. Granting ability, earnestness, and a thorough knowledge of business, the best man has a limit of cerebral power, and there is only a portion of the twenty-four hours in the day which can be devoted to work. To exceed the limit of cerebral power, and exceed the reasonable limit of hours of thought or business, by attempting the work of two or three men, is to court disaster sooner or later. Industry is to be prized. But hustling—so much admired and lauded in some quarters as the outward sign of genius and business success—is a fallacy of the first order. For one man who has made a trifling fortune out of it, a thousand have found their way into bankruptcy, if not ill-health, in which the mind is involved as well as the body. I see wrecks around me every day of men who have failed in life from attempting too much; from carrying too much sail; having too many irons in the fire. And I see other men who have concentrated on one or two things at first, and then added others gradually—with additional assistants—and thus step by step making a solid foundation for success and getting it.

IT IS NOT THE HUSTLER WHO SUCCEEDS, BUT THE MAN WHO CONCENTRATES, AND IMPORTS ORDER, METHOD, AND PROMPTITUDE INTO HIS PROFESSION OR BUSINESS.

In general business, retail concerns, where a great

variety of objects and interests have to be looked after and considered and an equally large variety of tastes to be met, all of which require attention in rapid succession, a marked degree of the power of abstract contemplation would be a hindrance. The salesman so endowed would be wholly out of place; for instance, an absent-minded dreamer—thinking of the dear-knows-what when he should be attending to the customer or the matter in hand. Men of this type are failures, because they are in the wrong place. They have not the alertness of mind and ability to give attention to matters requiring *immediate thought*. Such men—it matters little whether their salary be one or five pounds a week—get discharged as "no good." It would be a folly to imagine by paying the higher salary that one would get better service. The practical man of business has no room for dreaming philosophers and budding scientists—however useful they might be else-where—in his counting-house, back of his counters, or in his stores. A little less learning and more common sense will command his respect and obtain a larger salary. He wants men to do the work for which they are paid, to earn more if able. Men of sense do that; whatever latitude they may allow themselves outside business hours, they concentrate on the duties in hand while at work. These are the men that count. Competition or no competition, they are always in demand.

Intelligence, courage, firmness, and mental alertness are all exercised more thoroughly when the effort is put forth, with sincere determination, to DO ONE THING AT A TIME. That is concentration, and it will be seen from the previous lessons it can be cultivated. By aid of the breathing exercises, by the cultivation of deep breathing, by learning to keep the mouth shut, and other processes of self-control, much has and can be done to cultivate Will-power and concentration. While educating yourself by these processes, much more can be done by Non-comatose Auto-suggestion.

Having so many readers, all engaged in different pursuits, it is obvious that I cannot specialise a mode adapted to suit each particular temperament and employment. Still, much can be done. It is safe to say more young men fail from *lack of interest*—thoroughness in their work—than from any other cause. This means too often that they have plenty of interest, and concentration too—for other things. INTEREST ALWAYS CONCENTRATES.

To cultivate concentration, make it your business to have an interest in your work. WORK WHILE WORKING; PLAY WHEN PLAYING; REST WHEN RESTING; but don't mix things, and play, rest, and dream when you should be working. To do so is to court misfortune, and if in employment to get discharged; or if in business for yourself, to lack success. Earn your salary, or your success, by working for it at the right time. Many a man gets discharged for neglect of work, through "wool-gathering." He lacks self-respect, and, more than that, is dishonest. He has been aiming to get his salary without earning it. If concentration is essential in the master, it is demanded of the employee as a matter of right. The latter would do well on selfish lines—to say the least—to promote his own interests by attending to his duties while at them.

Concentration, order, method, and punctuality are associated in all successful business men. Take a very large class of men whom modern business methods have called into existence—advertising and insurance agents, canvassers, commission agents, and travellers— from high to low grades, from permanent to casual. Who are the men to succeed, and pass from the low to the high grade, from the casual to permanent employment? The men who start work by leaving their homes or offices without any definite plan; calling on some one at one end of the town, and then tramping off to the other, or perhaps dropping into a convenient " house of call " to see the papers, and partake of some " liquid refreshment," to lighten the tedium of their exhausting labours (?); or the men who have carefully arranged beforehand the order of their work—letters to be written, circulars despatched; the district to be worked; the different persons to be called on; the appointments made; the nature of the interview; WHAT THEY MEAN TO GET and HOW THEY MEAN TO GO ABOUT IT; having duly concentrated their minds on these points beforehand, they start out in the right spirit? There is no doubt whatever which of the two classes will succeed. The first, having no real interest and method in work, fail. The latter, meaning business, and working for it, SUCCEED. The first get the order to "get out," and the latter manage to "get in." The first get the door shut in their faces, and the latter *magnetically open them*—get a hearing and business done where the others fail. The first concentrate their minds on anything but work, and the latter on WHAT IS TO BE DONE: WHEN, NOW, AND HOW TO DO IT. THEY GET UP AND GET IT. IT IS YOUR GET-UP-AND-DO-IT MAN WHO SUCCEEDS ALL THE TIME.

What is true in the callings of the agent, canvasser, and traveller, is true in all departments of life. The orderly, prompt, systematic man, who makes himself master of his particular branch, is so far confident and self-reliant that he invites success and gets it. He invites confidence and influence, and gets it. He invites promotion and permanent employment, and gets it. He is on the outlook for opportunities, and gets them. He is not a hustler, but a thorough, clear-headed worker. What he takes in hand he carries through. What he is given to do he concentrates on and carries out to the best of his ability.

Next to want of the "power of continuity," as expressed in mental flightiness, unrest, and lack of proper interest, one finds in common therewith two pronounced features — LACK OF ORDER — INCLUDING METHOD, AND PROCRASTINATION.

Where these defects are ingrained—so to speak—and no reasonable steps are taken by the individual to remedy them, "ill-luck," as a matter of course, follows in their train. Of lack of Order, little need be said. Although it is a deplorable defect, it can be remedied.

The man who has intelligence enough to read these pages can improve himself IF HE SO WILLS. He is not to attempt desperately to remedy *all* his short-comings in a few days and then give up in despair. But take one defect at a time, give it attention for several days, and a new and better habit will be formed. The same may be said about procrastination. This bad habit can be cured like any other, where the evil is recognised and the proper means taken sincerely in hand.

As to want of Order, the fault may be in the man, in his parents, or in the circumstances under which he has spent most of his early years. From careful observation, I find that while all men are not endowed alike with the primary mental faculty of Order, none — save some idiots, weak-minded persons — are defective ; and the main reason for want of Order is to be found either in want of training in childhood, or self-training subsequently. Lack of Order, like want of punctuality, may be mainly traced to want of real interest, and to lack of discipline or true control of one's self.

The folly of well-meaning parents has a good deal to do with this defect. They allow their children to be careless and unmethodical in private life. They train (?) the children to depend on either their mother or servants —by the mother's orders—to DO things for the children, which the children should DO for themselves. The children lose their handkerchiefs; leave their toys about; throw their caps anywhere ; undress and throw their clothes on any chair or anywhere, going to bed. "The poor dears are so tired, you know"; and the mother or servants have the "order" to attend to. The children thus taught (?) depend on others to do for them that which they should have been instructed to do for themselves, this mistaken kindness going a long way, not only to hinder the development of Order in early life, but interfering with the proper and orderly development of that spirit of Independence and Self-reliance, so essential to success in after life.

The boy who is continually mislaying things, and who depends on his mother or the servants getting his cap, finding his handkerchief, putting away his books, finds himself handicapped in after life by his want of Order. He is perpetually losing his tools, his knife, his tobacco, and his money—at anyrate his money-making powers. He keeps an untidy desk, or if he has anything to do with anyone else's desk he leaves it littered. He has no sense of decency or the common courtesy which will leave things right for the favour conferred. All this carelessness must be a serious drawback to one in either a professional, constructive, or a commercial career. There are a few sensible men—of whom you, who read this lesson, may be one —painfully conscious of a want of order, and set about the remedy. There are others who are always losing their knives, umbrellas, etc., and who would lose their eye-teeth if they were not by Nature fully secured in their mouths. They also (to make their defect more certain, and possibly as an excuse for the bother and annoyance which they give to others) go about bemoaning their defect in this style:—

"Have you seen my knife?   I am always losing one."

"It is such a nuisance, but I can't help myself."

"I'm sure I have tried to remember, but I always forget," etc.

By this self-condolence they hypnotise themselves by Auto-suggestion in the confirmation of a bad habit. That is bad enough, but they by their excuses, self-commiseration, and fishing for sympathy, proclaim to the world "how utterly unreliable and untrustworthy they are." They may be well-meaning, possibly industrious, but they are generally fickle, unreliable, and not to be trusted.   Most certainly the men who are conscious of these defects in Order and memory, and who do not set about the CURE, are not to be trusted. Why?   Because they are too lazy to help themselves.

If they took half as much pains to cure themselves of this defect in Order, as they do to convince themselves that they cannot help themselves, they would cure the defect in a comparatively short time.   Let them start with a simple exercise of selecting a special place to put their hat or of making a practice of keeping their knife in a certain pocket.   As an Auto-suggestion exercise, the following will be of service: "Take the knife out, look at it, open it, close it, and then return it to that pocket.   Do this several times in succession, three or four times a day.   Repeat this two or three times, whenever using the knife privately, and in a short time there will be no lost knives."   From this it will become an easier matter to remedy some other defect in memory or in Order.

Want of Order is frequently associated with want of punctuality—procrastination, and it is almost certain that the man who has not the gumption to save his own time, and be in time to attend to his own interests, will waste the time and neglect the interests of his employers. It will be well to bear in mind that every step taken to improve Order will help to improve the Time sense—punctuality.

Procrastination, like lack of order, may be an ingrained defect. Some men appear born with a twist, and have an utter distaste for orderly and systematic work. They do not like to be "rung in" and "rung out," with special hours for work, food, and rest. Rest and recreation they are ready for at all times; but as for work, they will have none of it unless driven to it by unkind (?) relatives or an empty stomach. They appear to be born tired. They move in the direction of the least resistance or the current stream of their own undisciplined appetites and passions. They are ready to gratify these—at anyone's expense; but dig they won't, and to beg and impose they are not ashamed. Whether in high society or low, they are the non-producers, loafers, tramps, and ne'er-do-wells of the community. Yet even these, as we have seen—in the Army, in Labour Colonies, and by the means of other agencies—are quite capable of improvement, showing that there is less of "ingrained" defect, want of discipline, or culture, being the outstanding cause. A man living in tents or accustomed to " out-spanning " in the Veldt, to open doors and open fields all his life, may be excused if he forgets to shut a door after him when in England. This is not want of order, nor indicative of carelessness, but merely want of usage. Given a little time and practice, the newer and better habit can be formed. But the time and the practice must be given.

There is, however, in most men a love of ease, and a tendency to put off to to-morrow what should be done to-day; what should be done in the morning, to night; and every man who loves his manhood should wrestle with this defect and overcome it. It has been done, and can be done; and every person conscious of the weakness and the losses occasioned by want of order and by procrastination, can overcome these defects. Every step taken by these lessons to cultivate the WILL, develops courage, firmness, faith in self, is a step taken in the conquest of procrastination.

The procrastinator is invariably an unlucky man. He wonders and groans about his ill-luck, and attributes " all sorts " of undesirable qualities to the more fortunate. He is always philosophising, but industry, frugality, forethoughtfulness, are qualities which he does not prize. His ill-luck is due to a demoralised and un-disciplined state of mind in the first place, and to procrastination in the second place.

The late " Max O'Rell," who was a happy humorist, an indefatigable worker, and known to some of us as an able and charming lecturer, has said: " Luck means rising at six o'clock in the morning; living on a dollar a day if you can earn two; minding your own business, and not meddling with other people's. Luck means appointments you have never failed to keep; trains you have never failed to catch." There is a lot of shrewd sense in this, and the man who would be lucky should drop procrastination and drift, and put the foregoing methods promptly into practice.

Luck means taking advantage of opportunities; it means doing hard work when it has to be done and when it should be done. It means preparing the ground in winter, sowing in spring and summer, reaping in autumn, and not leaving to spring what should have been done in winter, to summer what should be done in spring, to autumn that which should have been attended to in summer; or to old age, to "by-and-by," that which should have been done in youth and manhood. The lucky man is just a sensible, sane, orderly, punctual, healthy, self-controlled man, of independent spirit, not afraid of hard work, who can save time as well as money, by planning wisely, looking ahead, and keeping a silent tongue in his head. Other people do the talking for him: "he is such a lucky man." He may not have been lucky all at once, but he has got into the way of it in time, by steadily and persistently practising the qualities placed to his credit. He does not talk about his successes, and he has sense enough to conceal his failures. One might do worse than follow his example.

To procrastinate means shirking work and the means

of success; for "Everything comes to the man who goes after things for which someone else is waiting." Procrastination means psychical blindness, inability to foresee and grasp what should be attended to ; it means inattention to the lessons of experience in which drifting and inattention have brought ill-luck. Procrastination is not only the thief of time, but of health, strength, fortune, happiness, success, love, respect, and every other good quality which endears a man to those who can treasure and appreciate worth.

The way to cure procrastination is not to think and worry about it, and regret, "If I had life to live over again, I would do so and so," but GET TO WORK NOW AND DO THAT WHICH SHOULD BE DONE. The things which should be done first, commence with them. There may be some leeway to make up. Don't worry about that. You cannot rectify the errors of a lifetime, but you can—by the way you order your life—avoid making more. Begin by forming a habit of being prompt to time in your office, of never missing your appointment, train, or boat. Prepare your interviews and journeys in advance. Do not leave things to the last minute. Leave nothing to others which you should attend to yourself. Better a minute or two too soon at your meeting, business, or railway station, than a second late. Don't procrastinate, except going to your electrocution. Don't bother about punctuality then. It will be attended to for you. Should you decide to procrastinate dying, by living a temperate, sensible, and orderly life, that defect can be overlooked. But living this life is just what the procrastinator fails to do. Show by control of yourself that you have regard for the well-being and comfort of your fellows; that order and punctuality are manly virtues which you prize. Your wife or housekeeper will smile thrice to her former once, when she finds you neither spoil the dinner nor her temper by being late to partake of what she has so carefully prepared for you. Disorderly and unpunctual beings are not only very selfish, but they are tactless, and certainly wanting in that attractive grace which is a feature in Personal Magnetism. A procrastinating, unpunctual man, "although said to be good-looking," is not a magnetic personality; he is not only too selfish and conceited to be attractive or desirable, but—matrimonially speaking—is not to be depended on to keep "the pot boiling." But I must pass on.

A procrastinating man is unsuccessful. One hour missed in the morning takes three in the afternoon to overtake, and then with considerable loss of energy, time, and possibly temper. That hour missed not only throws everything back, but just missed "Success" when it called. That hour lost, closed several doors of opportunity.

Rest assured that there is nothing so deteriorating physically, and demoralising mentally, as procrastination. If you are touched with it, get rid of it as you would a dangerous disease. It is certainly a serious mental malady. I cannot tell how much a man loses by procrastination, and how much he gains by doing things promptly and at the right time. You remember that paragraph you meant to cut out of the paper and did not? That letter you meant to write and did not, and lost a post, and a situation, or maybe lost a friend? You remember that fine train of thought you had on such a subject, and did not jot it down at the time, and lost it for ever? Be in Time; wait on Time; value Time; and you will never have occasion to waste breath, health, energy, and temper — Self-control — running after Time. The Self-reliant man is orderly and punctual; he is neat, spruce, and always UP TO TIME.

Want of interest, concentration, order, and punctuality may not be your trouble, but they are defects in character with many. Many a good position has been lost in consequence; many a concession, fortune, lost— as the battle was, for want of the nail in the right place and at the proper time. Much might be gained by the deliberate cultivation of concentration, order, and punctuality. You can help yourself by the use of a note-book, or one of the "Where is it?" order, a "commonplace book," a nest of drawers *in your head* as well as at your hand, where things can be properly put away for use at the right time. Without developing your powers you have been robbed of time, energy, application, efficiency, self-respect, and success. Do you want to improve? BEGIN NOW. NOW or NEVER. No more lost time for you; no more procrastination; no more waiting for something to turn up. You will start just now to turn up things for yourself. You will not wait for the mountain — of Influence and Success—to come to you; you are off to it. JUST NOW, RIGHT AWAY, START ON YOUR JOURNEY. DO IT NOW.

Take a suitable card, and have painted on it in luminous paint,

"DO IT NOW,"

and place that card in your bedroom where your eyes —when they open—will fall upon it. See the words; think over them; say them; and DO what they suggest.

IS IT THE PROPER TIME TO SLEEP? DO IT NOW.

IS IT THE PROPER TIME TO RISE? DO IT NOW.

TO PRACTISE AUTO-SUGGESTION? DO IT NOW.

TO TAKE BREAKFAST AND EAT PROPERLY? DO IT NOW.

IS IT TIME TO LEAVE HOME FOR OFFICE OR APPOINT-MENT? DO IT NOW.

You will be all the better for rising in time to be well groomed, and to eat your breakfast properly and get a cheerful send-off, before you get to your train, 'bus, desk, bench, counter, or round of appointments. Keep the plan of DO IT NOW before your mental vision as well as practising it during the day.

See yourself thorough, wideawake, efficient, obliging, giving prompt attention—in a manly, wideawake, and self-reliant way—to the work which lies near you. Live up to your vision. " Have a purpose in life . . . . and having it, throw such strength of mind and muscle into thy work as has been given thee."

These lessons will help you to apply yourself to ONE THING AT A TIME; to be patient, thorough, and painstaking; to be orderly, punctual, and trustworthy; to keep your thoughts centred on the object, purpose, person, etc., till the end desired be achieved. Put the directions in this chapter into practice.

DO IT NOW.

CHAPTER XIV

SUGGESTION AND ITS APPLICATION

" There is no endowment in man or woman that is not tallied in
    you.
There is no virtue, no beauty, in man or woman, but as good in
    you.
No pluck, no endurance in others, but as good in you.
No pleasure waiting for others, but equal pleasure waits for you."
                                                    WHITMAN.

To understand Suggestion and its power in either a
therapeutic (health restorative) or in a mental development (intellectual culture, will-power, self-reliant
character or integrity) sense, it will be necessary to say
something about Suggestion, its application by others,
and its self-application—or Auto-suggestion—which in
my opinion is the most helpful of all. By its agency
we have at hand a remedy which we can apply to ourselves.

The brain—including the entire nervous organisation
—is the organ of the mind, and the medium by which
we are—in present physical modes of existence—related
to two worlds : that which is without us, " the NOT ME,"
and to that within us, " the ME," or the world of
thought, consciousness, and sub-consciousness, and all
which that includes. By the brain, through the organs

of the sense, we are related to the world without, and by mentation or thought processes—whether these may be momentary impulses, fragmentary and apparently incoherent thoughts, or the deepest conscious and sub-conscious operations—to the world within. The world within us is a world of infinite possibilities, and is in touch with the Infinite, and our Psychic-Self is sustained by the Inspiration of the All Good, as our bodies are by the inspiration of life and by the sustaining forces of the air breathed and by the kindly fruits of the earth. Our external conscious life is made all the more delight-ful and enjoyable by the exercise of our own powers, such as the tillage of the soil and other modes of labour which enhance our powers. Man does not live by bread alone. He lives in two modes of existence, and for each he requires suitable aliment, and in both cases the food he labours for will be the sweetest and most nourishing.

The subtle relationship of mind and brain has occupied the closest study of the deepest thinkers in modern times, from Reid, Stewart, Hamilton, and Gall onwards to Gates. The materialistic psychologist and the spiritualistic psychologist have each in their way dealt with this subject, and what has been a source of complexity and deep research and controversy to them need not take up much of your time. In this life we know nothing of mind apart from its instruments—the brain and the nervous system. The brain being the organ of the mind, upon its integrity and health, its vigour and the development of its various centres, the

15

fullest or best manifestation of mind depends. Every
thought, emotion, and impulse, as well as the very
highest process of thought, produces immediate effects
on and in the brain substance. It can also be safely
said that every operation of the mind has a twofold
effect—mental and physical. Thus thought on the
conscious side is that of feeling, emotion, perception,
and judgment; sensation the physical expression.
Certain thoughts repeated produce certain sensations,
and like sensations produce or bring into play thoughts
of which we are conscious. By the brain we are related
to our body and its environment, constituting the NOT
ME or the world without. The ME, per the brain, is informed through our senses, which are our ordinary
avenues of knowledge. The senses, while having each
their own distinct functions, are reciprocal as aids to
knowledge. We receive impressions— vibrations —
visual, auditory, sensory, etc., through appropriate
sense-channels. Should, however, one sense be weak
or defective, we may still gain information by the
agency of the other sense-organs and their centres in
the brain, conveyed from thence to the cortical cells of
the anterior lobes; *but when and how a vibration is trans-
lated into a thought of which we are conscious, is a process
of which we are utterly ignorant,* and can only surmise
by the aid of the Psychic hypothesis. If one organ or
centre of the brain be weak or defective—notwithstanding that each has its own distinctive function—
we can in a measure bring about an adjustment by
cultivating that centre and bringing into play its latent

energy by the co-operation of other centres, which are also stimulated by us in the course of exercise or education. We improve the mind by special exercises.

It is evident that while no two brains are alike, and no two persons are either temperamentally, mentally, or psychically similar, it is also clear that everyone can—by "attendance on Moderation," attention to health, ordinary hygiene, diet, *habits*, modes of living—materially enhance or improve their brain powers, and through culture, mental gymnastics—Auto-suggestion—develop powers of Self-reliance, and other capacity for usefulness and success. If this improvement be impossible, all preaching, teaching, education, and even the very idea of responsibility, is vanity and vexation of spirit. But we know different; it is ours to improve, and ours is the responsibility. Progression is the pathway of the wise. It is for us to take that way.

A brief outline of habits—repeated modes of thought and action—has already been given. I only refer to this outline in calling attention to the fact that by Suggestion, new habits—automatic and sub-conscious modes—can be created and all mental powers enhanced. I have dealt pretty fully with suggestion in my other published books; still, a little space may be set aside here for a brief outline of this subject. The study of hypnotism clearly emphasises that suggestion is merely the putting into deliberate and conscious practice—for a wise, definite, and useful purpose—that which most of us are doing unconsciously for ourselves every day. For instance, *as we think, we are*. As we think furtively,

haphazardly, incompletely, procrastinatingly, passion-
ately, impulsively—influenced thereto by undisciplined
emotions, appetites, and sensations—we are failures
and deteriorate—are the playthings of this and that
obstinate storm—passion, anger, hysteria, and lust—of
ill-regulated thought, instead of progressing to honour
and true manhood as the years go by. That is one
picture.

Under the influence of higher thoughts, " which come
from above," through the coronal centres of the brain,
and from " the *double* within us which is wiser than
we ": thoughts suggested to us by wise, pure-minded,
and sympathetic companionship, suitable books, study,
education, combined with increasing self-determination
to improve and advance—all things in our environment
will become suggestions of Self-help, warning, advancement, and progress. What in the former picture would
be inducements or suggestions of evil, in this latter
aspect of mind become examples of something to avoid ;
suggestions to us to earnestly progress and live our
fullest, truest, and best life. Thus what, in ordinary
experience, would be suggestive of evil to one person
would be suggestive of good to another. Some go
through life, gay, frivolous, and self-gratifying, or most
probably seeing evil and misery in everything and
everybody ; therefore live and think accordingly—
suggest themselves into an evil and unhappy state of
being. Others, again, do not so learn life ; *they look for*
the good, think it, and aim at possession, and get it. That
is the judicious course to pursue.

In estimating our fellows, in thinking of our friends
—none so wretched and abandoned that they do not
latently possess an infinite store of that which is good
—let us think the best; let us with kindly thoughts
uplift and cheer them, and *let these thoughts* raise
humanity in our eyes, and also *be suggestions to ourselves*
to advance in the direction of a sounder and more level-
headed manhood.

If the day be dull, do not let that affect you. Look
for the " bit of blue " (in the sky of your mental and
spiritual state) which is sure to be there, and think of
it and not of the leaden, drab, dull, and miserable aspect
of things. If you do not see that " bit of blue " in the
sky, have faith that it is there and that you will see it
presently—AND YOU WILL.

In business and in domestic affairs—while using sane
judgment in the one and sympathetic relationship in
the other—look for that which is best, and you will be
a better, brighter, more desirable, and a more successful
man in consequence. As master, your influence—not
being that of an eternally carping, dissatisfied critic, and
hard to please—will command better service from your
employees. As a servant you will render better service
—even under difficult circumstances. As husband and
father, you can be a little blind—sometimes with great
advantage—while your kindness, patience, and love will
be factors which will help to make home, home indeed.

The wind, weather, food, persons, circumstances, and
almost every internal sensation are suggestions of evil,
ill-luck, and misfortune to one man, while full of all

that is good to another. When I say good, I mean useful and necessary. And the difference really depends on how we adapt ourselves to our environment. One man—always a grumbler—thinks if he had the regulation of the Universe; the making of the laws of his country; the dividing of other people's possessions, and the hanging of some people, he would be a happy man. Poor fellow! Another will adjust himself to his surroundings, and while doing his level best, will keep his eye keen for opportunities and thus make the best of himself and them. The first is mean, miserable, a failure, and a chronic specimen at that. The latter is a success, in whatever be his sphere. The first looks to that which is without him for Health, Wealth, and Success; the second to himself to gain all three. The latter is the wiser of the two. So much for suggestions arising from ordinary experience. Like the gentleman who wrote " prose " all his life and was not aware of it, we are making " suggestions " to ourselves all through life—for good or ill—and many of us are not aware of that. WHAT WE SUGGEST TO OURSELVES (to-day) WE BECOME (to-morrow).

Psycho-therapeutic Suggestion, which has been pretty fully dealt with in my other works, will only call here for a brief remark or two. In medical practice, for instance, suggestion is indirectly made to the patient by the ability, presence, and actual health of the medical attendant—often without being aware of it. His advice and his medicines are the pivots on which the faith, confidence, and experience of the

patient turn.   Nature — the subconscious forces —
(aroused and stimulated by hope, mental action—of the
conscious self—is helped by these processes) CURES.
*The treatment is much more effective when the physician
is aware of, and deliberately makes his advice, suggestions
towards cure.* But in all cases where the medical
practitioner is a healthy, energetic, sympathetic man,
possessed of Self-reliance, he begets confidence and
trust in his patient, whether he practises consciously
therapeutic suggestions or not.   From this there is but
another step, that of the employment of Therapeutic
Suggestion—according to the best methods of hypnotic
practice—to cases in which ordinary medical procedure
would be ineffectual. Suggestion, in the latter sense.
should be employed—with the patient's consent only.
The operator can, in addition to the hypnotic suggestions,
advise the patient to adopt such and such courses
as may be deemed useful for recovery, also help
him or her to carry out that advice, and therefore
practically aid the patient to help himself. If certain
practices—erroneous habits of eating and drinking—or
aught else have been the means of inducing ill-health,
and, therefore, the means of hindering cure, these
practices are in due time cut off and better and wiser
modes inculcated.   Psycho - therapeutic or healing
suggestions, in addition to the foregoing aids, are
given to the patient subsequent to the production of an
acquiescent or suggestible state. In this state the
patient's mental operations are reduced to a minimum ;
his mind is then concentrated on the special suggestion

which the operator means to have incorporated in the patient's subconscious self, and eventually to be the mainspring of the patient's improved health, conduct, will-power, usefulness, and what not. In the foregoing, we have an outline of Suggestion in Medical Hypnotic Practice; but in the next phase of Suggestion—that of Non-comatose Suggestion—we learn to operate on ourselves.

In Comatose Suggestion, a state of sleep or that of approximating to sleep is induced before the healing suggestions or commands are given. In Non-comatose Auto-suggestion you are not asleep, although in a passive state, and you are conscious of the suggestions which you make to yourself. Sleep when it comes does not hinder the success of the operation in the waking state, as the subconscious self—by means of appropriate media in the organisation—carries out the operation. As a simple illustration, suppose, on retiring to bed, you know you have to rise at an unusually early hour to catch a train, or enter upon some duty or other; although you have not been in the habit of rising before, say, eight in the morning, yet if you will keep the matter before your mind's eye last thing at night, before falling to sleep, you will awaken at two, three, or at any other hour you have determined upon. What are the causes of your success? You are in earnest; you have impressed the necessity upon yourself during the day, *but especially at night*, when in a receptive state—the borderland of sleep,—and you have awakened at the hour appointed in response to the request or suggestion made by your (conscious) self, earnestly and thoroughly to your other (subconscious) self, and have reaped the reward. There is no ordinary mental defect which you, yourself, cannot cure. In my experience, I have helped correspondents, the wide world over, to CURE most serious defects in themselves, by getting them to extend the above principle of suggestion to themselves.

You will also know now, as the result of actual experience — if you have carried out the simple exercises already given in the foregoing hints to you —how much you can help yourself. You have been, in fact, practising Non-comatose Auto-suggestion in a way, and now know how to help yourself. If suggestions from others are potent factors in health and disease, suggestions to ourselves are more effective and important. *We are nearest in touch with ourselves.* Even suggestions from others do not affect us *unless accepted and believed in by ourselves.* What we think, we become, on ordinary conscious and subconscious planes of life.

It is not my intention to take up space with the treatment of disease, although no more powerful agent than Suggestion can be applied to that end. For instance, taking two ordinary and, alas! too common complaints, chronic constipation and sleeplessness, these have been cured by Suggestion when all other methods have been tried in vain. The foregoing diseases, or rather symptoms, indicating deeper underlying causes, would, owing to the relationship and interaction of mind and brain, hinder the proper mentation or manifestation of the mind. The intellect would be dull, and listlessness, or perhaps irritability of disposition, be exhibited. Hope or buoyancy shown at its lowest ebb; various brain centres being either poisoned by disease-laden blood, or ineffectually nourished, would be as incapable of exercising their functions, as a decrepit and half-starved cart-horse would be of hauling a loaded dray. The sufferer, while willing to do good, finds that evil is present with him—so long as these defects are not remedied. *Indeed, the thoughts, feelings, and sensations experienced and dwelt upon*—unless removed by careful, repeated, and steady Auto-suggestion—*would only exaggerate the diseased bodily states.* But, as I have said, the object of these hints in Auto-suggestion is not so much the cure of disease—although the groundwork for that is not neglected in these pages—as their application (in true self-help earnestness) to improve one's mental powers. For instance, the cure of nervous timidity; self-consciousness; want of confidence; mental abstraction; procrastination, or some other akin defect, which is a hindrance to one's progress in life and often a stumbling-block in the way of well-meaning mortals. Taking for granted that you want to cultivate Self-reliance, you have in Non-Comatose Suggestion the remedy and the means.

Professor Elmer Gates, late of the Smithsonian Institute, Washington, D.C., U.S.A., and one of the foremost practical psychologists of the day, has said :—

"Bad and unpleasant feelings create harmful chemical

products in the body which are physically injurious. Good, pleasant, benevolent and cheerful feelings create beneficial chemical products which are physically health-ful. These products may be detected by chemical analysis in the perspiration and secretions of the individual. More than forty of good and as many of bad have been detected. Suppose half a dozen men in a room. One feels depressed, another remorseful, another ill-tempered, another jealous, another cheerful, another benevolent. Samples of their perspiration are placed in the hands of the psycho-physicist. Under his examination they reveal all these emotional con-ditions distinctly and unmistakably."

The foregoing, which we accept, and all our whole arguments tend to prove, should be a further incentive to back unpleasant thoughts, and learn the mastery of self, if only on the grounds that this wiser conduct contributes to health and physical well-being. Self-examination will show to most who care to go in for that sort of introspection, that they think in grooves, and sometimes very fearful and desponding grooves, and are thus literally devitalising and poisoning the system. They are also arresting the metabolic processes, and the functions of the vegetative or sympathetic nerve centres, and all this contributes to ill-looks, premature decay, and death. Even when it is not so bad as this, Fear, Temper, Irresolution, as well as " our pleasant vices are made the instruments to punish us." Self-examination will also show that bright and cheerful thinking, kind and pleasant thoughts, calm and intellectual decision, also make their own grooves, and bring into play a more perfect metabolism—that subconscious operation by which air, water, food, etc., are converted into vital sustaining processes—blood and muscle—and impurities and effete matters are eliminated from the system. Beauty and comeliness of the outward form are enhanced, and health, strength, and long life are the concomitants of right thinking. In fact, all our mental states are mirrored in the face and body. All these states can be regulated and controlled, and this is the chief object in all self-culture, self-control procedure, whether this is carried out by the ordinary processes of self-regulation or by the more deliberate methods of Non-comatose Suggestion, by which one sets oneself a deliberate task, and is not satisfied till able to perform it.

There is abundant evidence that men who have lived unwisely up to middle life and later, have succeeded to live worthily later on. Self-examination has led to a different outlook, a conviction of necessity, a finer and better mode of thought; and that change has been evidenced in the individual, yes, and also in his environment. IT IS NEVER TOO LATE TO MEND. All can improve. While there is life there is hope. But the mending must commence now—to-day—not to-morrow. And HOPE must be exercised now, and all can thus rebuild their brains and remodel their own minds at will. And if not easier, it is as easy to improve the mind as the body by exercise. Physical culture experts will show you how to develop this or that muscle where weak,[1] and the suggestions which have been thrown out in these pages have all been to one end — to enable those who care to improve those faculties or mental muscles which are weak in the mind. As the mind is exercised the brain will undergo correlative changes. In a short time the physiological substance will adapt itself to the mental processes. By Non-comatose Suggestion we have the means of proper exercise at hand, and as you have intelligence enough to read these pages, you possess power enough and all the means at hand necessary to make your mind progressive, pure, cheerful, definite, firm, self-reliant, Masterly. " I WILL " and " I CAN " will be no idle boast, but facts.

I have referred to Auto-suggestion. It will be as well to explain more in detail what is meant. " Auto " means " self," and " Suggestion " really means " impression," and thus Auto-suggestion is a mode of procedure by which we produce impressions in ourselves. The impression is one which may arise in one's mind from something external to self. Thus, when the dinner-bell rings, that is a suggestion which stimulates appetite, suggests hunger, and the need of food, all of which were non-existent before the sound of the bell. Impressions can be made on self through the other channels of sense. Instances of this can be readily called to mind when once you get to thinking on the

---

[1] The Key of Success, even in physical training, is to keep the mind on the special muscle you seek to develop by one or several exercises which you are employing to that end.

theme. But it is not generally known that while Auto-suggestions are used unconsciously, they can also be employed, consciously and deliberately, for a definite purpose.

Unconscious Auto-suggestion works good or ill *as it is directed*. And mark, please, it is within our power and direction. We are always receiving impressions and also creating them ; but the conscious employment of them becomes a high art and a fine art. Before we touch upon this conscious employment, let the mind dwell on the evidences we have from the pages of history, in religious experiences, and in our own common experience. History records some ninety cases of *stigmata*—cases of certain religiously minded devotees, such as St Francis of Assisi (Sept. 15, 1224), St Catherine of Siena, or the nun Veronica Giuliana, whose bodies, through the devout contemplation of their minds, became marked with the images of Christ and the tragedy of the Cross. The materialistic Protestant mind may reject all such occurrences, no matter how well testified ; but the equally materialistic mind versed in the science of hypnotism can accept the evidence of the power of the mind over the body, because such power has been demonstrated by experimentation.

Miraculous healing, which the Church of Rome has always accepted and never denied, has been amply testified to, and is a further evidence of the power of the mind over the body. Of course, the cures have been attributed to the power of God working through

His servants; and we know scientifically that the power of God and His servants was the human mind and its subconscious powers aroused to action by faith, fear, or devotion, and possibly fanned and encouraged by religious rites. In all ages there have been cures at various shrines and in the presence of relics—false and true. Of miraculous healing of this sort, I will note two instances. Bambino—the image of the Infant Jesus—is said to possess the power to cure disease. This little jewelled and somewhat tawdry figure is carried to the houses of wealthy patients in Rome who may be suffering with dangerous diseases—diseases which have baffled medical skill—and these have been cured with miraculous so-called results. The piles of crutches at Lourdes and Trèves, and at sacred wells in Wales or at the Knock in Ireland, are ample testimony to genuine cures which have taken place at these resorts. But we are no less familiar with cures wrought by votaries of Christian Science and other cults, these cures having their basis in Suggestion. In fact, to use the language of Dr Saleeby, a well-known medical authority, "The cures wrought by Christian Science are real cures. Faith-healing is a fact. Neither faith nor Mrs Eddy can remove mountains—or kill a bacillus —but mind can act on mind. Terrible maladies exist which the united wisdom of every physician on the earth might be impotent to affect, but which would yield instantly and finally to the nonsensical jabbering of an immoral imbecile, *if only the patient's mind were affected thereby*. These are scientific facts, and as important as the infectiousness of cholera, the germ causation of tuberculosis, or the triumphs of Listerian surgery." In the foregoing the language is strong, but it is a tardy admission of the power, not merely of suggestion, but of Auto-suggestion or the power of the mind on and in oneself. It is no doubt repugnant to the medical mind that an "unqualified" person—Christian Scientist, Mental Scientist, Catholic Priest, Protestant Layman, Hypnotist or Magnetist—should cure disease. The person cured does not mind the objection. The fact remains that the attitude of the " mind " invites disease and likewise the attitude of the mind cures, whatever the predisposing agency—Faith in God, self, or some fellow-creature. Bacillus or no bacillus, the awakened mind has cut short the course of a fever, cured paralysis, chronic rheumatism, and a host of diseases which no honest physician would claim as having a basis in a neurotic diathesis. The young and rising physician who recognises the action of the patient's mind in all diseases, and the action of his own mind on the mind of his patient, in the treatment of disease, will be the successful physician in the near future.

Faith and hope have in some cases aroused the necessary mental action. We see that religious exercises have intensified it, and have produced cures which have baffled medical skill. By hypnotism remarkable results have been produced. Under mental intensity something akin to *stigmata* has been produced; blisters have been created by an impression conveyed to the patient's mind that such would be the case. But apart from all this we have the evidence of observers and men of science, medical and lay, that neither religion nor hypnotism is the sole cause of all these " Miros," or wonders in the way of cure. *The action of the patient's mind on himself being the principal factor.*

AS YOU THINK, SO YOU WILL BE

There is no help like self-help, and Auto-suggestion is one of the modes by which this can be most satisfactorily carried out. Such as when a man says to himself, " I am deficient in moral courage. I must overcome this, and I will"; and then sets himself to the task of growing in grace and in moral strength. Or, possibly he finds himself deficient in some special line of knowledge to fit him for a certain post. He forthwith gets the necessary books and instruments, and deliberately sets aside a portion of his (perhaps limited) leisure time, and day after day masters that deficiency, and is able to take the post offered, or, perchance, take promotion in some higher branch of his own profession, trade, or calling, as the case may be. He says, " I WILL AND I CAN," and proceeds forthwith to put his assurance and his knowledge into practice. Well, that is Auto-suggestion and its proof. There is nothing very occult and mystic in that ; except it be in the subconscious operations of the mind, which are becoming more thoroughly investigated and more fully understood to-day.

Once get it clearly into your mind that your menta-

tion—thought—is both an actual and a potential force
for good or ill, and you will have a firm foundation
on which to build your Auto-suggestion practice.
While it is quite true that the state of the body, and
the action of the weather (for that matter) on the
body, reacts on the mind, the influence is insignificant
to that of the Mind—thought—on the body, states of
health or want of the latter.   It has been abundantly
proved by the remarkable effects of fear, anger, envy,
anxiety, and worry and other modes of emotion and
passion on the state of that body.   Fear of paralysis
has produced it.   And fear is the fertile source of an
infinite variety of diseases.   Fear has been known to
arrest vital processes, turn the hair white in a night,
and the fear of death has resulted in death.   A child
has been poisoned at the breast because the mother has
had a fit of temper.   And we all know that fear, depression, has arrested the course of digestion.   Dr Tuke,
an eminent authority in psychological, pathological, and
hypnotic research, declares that mental causation lies
at the basis of insanity, idiocy, paralysis of various
muscles and organs, profuse perspiration, cholera,
jaundice, skin diseases, and many other allied troubles.
All passions, selfish thoughts, lust, avarice, jealousy, and
anger translate themselves into physical or bodily
forms of expression.   They do more than this: they
mould the body on these lines, and in time the most
beautiful face and the most perfect human form will
be disfigured and degraded by them.   The blood will
be rendered impure, and the whole system will suffer;

anæmia, erysipelas, and eczema and their allied phases, are some of the modes of expression of this mental debasement. Religious ideas, which give erroneous conceptions of the Supreme, by which one is filled with unworthy thoughts towards one's fellow-men, also degrade and debase the physical organisation. Every mental state becomes pictured in the body ; this is an infallible truth sustained by the experiences of mankind. All men, however, do not notice this gradual deterioration by the dwelling on and the constant repetition of impure and degrading thought. But it is there, and there is no getting away from it. The MIND TRANSLATES ITSELF INTO FLESH AND BLOOD. It may be that some cannot read these signs of the mind's operations in the human features, and in the health of the organism, but they are there all the same even if they remain undiscovered " till the secrets of all hearts be revealed."

While it is true that there is so much chronic suffering, misery, and wretchedness in life, which is not only acquired but handed down, so that it is a wonder that there are so many with comparatively harmonious thoughts and perfectly healthy bodies, it is also true that this wretchedness and suffering is abnormal. It was evidently intended — from the very constitution of man—that harmonious thoughts and healthy bodies should be man's normal state. This is revealed to us by man's constitution. He is endowed with a moral, spiritual, and intellectual nature; this he seems to have overlooked while giving way to evil

thoughts, impulses, passions, and the gratification of
the animal appetites in various ways — weaknesses
which have been denounced by the wisest and best
thinkers in all ages, who have either intuitively
thought out or have been inspired to think out and
speak of such matters. A healthy mind and body is
man's normal state in this world; but, unfortunately, he
has sought out and grovelled in other states of mind,
and has made ill-health the apparently normal state of
mankind. The dawn is at hand, and we see those here
and there who peer through the coming light and see
that "a harmonious mind and a healthy body, with a
long, honourable, and useful life on earth, are to be
had for the asking."

A writer whom I do not know expressed himself to
the following effect :—

" Dwell upon your discouragements, and you multiply
their shadows until everything grows so dark that you
cannot see the divine face of success which is smiling
into your eyes from the very midst of your endeavours.
Discouragement never builded anything. Cheerful
confidence is the great architect building cottages and
cathedrals of business career. The great believers are
always the great achievers. Believe in the divinity of
yourself and the divinity of your business, and the two
of you will work one success. Get at the very soul of
your business and at the very soul of yourself, which
is always yourself at your best. However the seeming,
that is a great enough centre to achieve your honest
desire ; even the acorn is a great enough centre to

achieve God's honest idea of an oak. I am sure that God at His best meets the acorn at its best, and that is the only reason why oaks greaten in our fields and on our hills. Smile at your business, and it will smile back again. Follow the light of that smile, and yours are the ears that will hear it laugh in the large leagues of fulfilled desire."

What this writer so quaintly expresses is wonderfully true in all departments of life. Bring the brightness and joy, the sweetness and light that are within you into play, and you will find the response in greater harmony of mind, more perfect bodily conditions; and this is not all: greater success in work, business, religion—in a word, LIFE.

So far we have been talking of Auto-suggestion without formalism. We are dealing with the influence of the mind, not only over and in the body, but in the affairs of life, character, business, everything which makes life worth living.

We have noticed some of the evils which arise through unconscious mental suggestion, and the good which arises from conscious suggestions given to ourselves with a definite good object in view. "Smile at your business (friend, wife, child), and it will smile back at you." Speak with a smile in your voice, and you will tone down difficulties. "A soft answer turneth away wrath." In many ways this procedure of quietly and deliberately applying thought to create good impressions in yourself will arise in your own mind. Suppose you get a physical impression that the day is raw and cold, and you are depressed in consequence, or think you are, which is just the same. You say to those you meet, " It's a cold, raw day," instead of a cheery " Good day," or " Good morning," as the case may be. You are acquiescing in the former state of feeling and fixing it so as to feel colder than necessary and more miserable than you should. If you add (to yourself), " I am not feeling so well to-day—this weather is very unhealthy," you are not only making yourself a slave to your emotions, but actually allowing yourself to drift into a morbid state, simply because the sky is a bit overcast and the day is a bit colder than usual.

Give the thoughts a higher turn, and admit that all kinds of weather subserve some good and useful purpose, and that you are aware that you can more or less protect yourself against what, for you, may be inclement weather, by either more work or extra clothing, and, moreover, by a cheerful attitude turning your thoughts in a higher and brighter direction, so that you respond to those who greet you dolefully—" It's a good day."—" It's seasonable weather."—"We'll have brighter weather for this."—" It is a good day." With such words—uttered with cheery, optimistic emphasis—you repel the animal sensation of mere cold and depression. You not only triumph over these apparent inconveniences, but your attitude thereto uplifts and disciplines your mind, and directs it into proper and useful channels, in which there is no time to waste in profitless thoughts and useless repinings.

It is said that we cannot control our thoughts. That

is untrue. They will certainly be chaotic if no effort is made to control them, and will be coloured by our sensations and by a thousand and one influences; but with the effort we can make them what we please and direct them into the channels we think best. All this cannot be done at once, but step by step it CAN and WILL be ACHIEVED, if we are in real earnest. It is for us to decide whether our thoughts shall be undisciplined, chaotic, disorderly, inharmonious, and tinged with malice, vanity, self-conceit, fear, lust, or other passionate tendencies or weakness; or, on the other hand, whether we shall see to it that they shall make for health, harmony, cheerfulness, happiness, peace, love, purity, strength, moral courage, and manly worth. This can be done and is done daily by all who take life here on loan and mean to make the best of it.

"I AM WELL!"

"I am ready and willing!"

"I am bright and energetic!"

"I am reposeful, quiet, and thoughtful!"

"I am strong!"

"I and my mind are one!"

"I am, and because I AM, I govern my body!"

St Paul puts it in the language of his soul-awakened consciousness, "I keep my body in subjection," etc., etc.

All these, then, are Auto-suggestions. These and all other Suggestions esteemed necessary — given to oneself, in suitably receptive state—repeated and re-repeated, acted on and lived up to, become incorporated in self, and become our second nature, and our stronger nature, because really more in harmony with our constitution.

Auto-suggestion, however, really means, *those impressions which we create in self, when we are in a susceptible state.* We have seen what thought does without any conscious direction—that is, without thinking for a moment of the effects of those thoughts, good or bad, on ourselves. It is now for us to realise what thought will do for us, when deliberately utilised for self-improvement—by adding, in fact, to our faith the knowledge of practical experience.

I have suggested to you—for many reasons—that you were to eat less, drink more, and practise deep breathing. All these things were Auto-suggestions towards self-improvement in health and in self-control. I also suggested to you that you should go to bed a little earlier, and possibly lie a little longer, and, above all, that you should get at least half an hour's rest— real physical rest—in the afternoon. I urged this because, by so doing, you—who have been and are such a strenuous worker—would give your nervous system more vitality and pith, and your brain powers more vigour for the manifestation of thought. All this is good, but I had another object in view, and that was that you should secure some moments of absolute privacy for silence and reflection and the practice of Auto-suggestion in an orderly, systematic, and more effective way than any which you have accomplished as yet. All former procedure which you have adopted has been leading up to this.

CHAPTER XV

NON-COMATOSE AUTO-SUGGESTION ; PHYSICAL MODES

"A really great man must have courage and perseverance, independence of mind and strong convictions, a breadth and depth of sympathy, largeness of soul, an unbending will and power to guide people and yet to control them."—THE ARCH-BISHOP OF CANTERBURY.

I PROPOSE to give, in an informal way, a few cases which have been successfully treated by the agency of Non-Comatose Auto-suggestion. In every instance, none were amenable to medical treatment, and yet, whatever the peculiar mental disturbance or idiosyncrasy—whether traceable to ill-health, *bias* of temperament, unfriendly suggestion, habits of thought, etc.— all have proved amenable to Auto-suggestion. Even the most difficult, from having their physical basis in the nervous organisation, and although warped and exaggerated by ignorance, fear, and other phases of ill-regulated self-suggestion, *were, under more enlightened circumstances—instruction*—cured by Auto-suggestion.

The human mind has its limitations, no doubt— limitations which arise from various causes, such as, for example, the limits of the physical organisation, brain development, health or disease ; but the greatest limitation of all is more apparent than real. It arises from our failure to understand ourselves, whereby not one tithe of our mental powers are reasonably developed, educated, or exercised. And while this is true, there are further hindrances which arise from ignorance of the finer forces and powers of the subconscious self and its machinery (in the vegetative, involuntary, and automatic nerve-centres in brain and body), which have consequently been neglected, and which can be called into play, and disciplined by the educated intellect, and by the persistent direction—willing—of the ordinary conscious mind.

But, please notice, while mind has its limitations, no one can tell or know what these really are. What most men think they know, are only their own limitations in thought or experience. And it is the "fear" arising therefrom which controls them, and not the limitations. For the moment their limitations are seriously tackled, they vanish like mist before the morning sun. I believe, although I cannot prove it, that the human mind is infinite and eternally progressive, and is only limited in its expression by its physical instruments and environment. Even these are not beyond our control. As I have already made clear, we can improve the brain power by health and mental exercise, while experience teaches we can do much to improve our circumstances and change our environments. In the majority of cases, the limits which most men apprehend, or think to exist, have been proved groundless.

Take a case of obsession. A gentleman called upon me, dominated or possessed by "a fixed idea." He was an intelligent man, and held a responsible post, which he was afraid he would lose. He had the misfortune to witness a sailor cut his throat while in a drunken passion. The scene then witnessed, with all its horrid ghastliness—the rushing blood and the rolling eyes of the dying man—became pictured, so to speak, in this man's brain. This fixed picture obsessed him; it was obtruded upon him in his employment, in his public and private life, penetrated his dreams, and unnerved him. His work was imperfectly done. He was making frequent mistakes. Under advice, tonics, nervines, and stimulants were resorted to, but instead of benefiting him, they merely helped to confirm the obsession. This was a limitation of the mind indeed, and added to that was the almost hopeless belief that he was incapable of doing anything for himself.

Simple hygienic directions were given in breathing exercises, in drinking, eating, bathing, and they proved physically beneficial—all being indirect modes of Auto-suggestion. Then when he realised that he could do something for himself, and that the persistent carrying out of the breathing exercises not only benefited him physically, but in a measure diverted his mind from the horrid vision, I placed him on a graduated course of Auto-suggestions, and thus, with the physical improvement and gradual change of direction to the mind, the obsession was exorcised. The memory of the scene was not by any occult power blotted out, *but the power of* that mental picture to unman and harass was destroyed for ever. This was not all, for in the process of Self-treatment this gentleman practically rebuilt himself into a wiser, stronger, and better man. He discovered himself.

Another form of obsession—so far not tractable to medicinal treatment, but distinctly amenable to suggestive therapeutics—is that of "hearing voices." As a rule, the sufferer obtains little sympathy from his fellows, and many who should know better significantly tap their foreheads when they hear of these cases. Nothing is so disconcerting to an intelligent man as to find that he is harassed by "voices"—voices which appear to be directed by intelligences—in the body and out—and which are heard by the patient, damning, reviling, threatening, and urging suicide as the only way of escape. The voices—which are subjective— seem to be intimately acquainted with his affairs, and so, whether wholly illusory, or having a foundation in fact through some cerebral defect in the auditory centres, they are obsessing. The patient often becomes physically deteriorated, and all pleasure in life vanishes. He is terrorised by this experience. Medical treatment, helpful in many ways, seems to be valueless here. Yet in such a case as this, suggestion steps in and cures. It is better thus, than that the gaol, asylum, or the bottom of some pool should be the end of such a sufferer.

One can imagine the joy experienced—not that the voices cease at once; but the patient *ceases to fear them* in the first place, and is eventually rid of them in the second place, and lastly discovers himself in increased physical health and mental balance. Such are some of the things which Non-Comatose Auto-suggestion has been able to accomplish.

A medical student had foolishly contracted a drug habit. That habit obsessed him, until he had learned to cure himself by Auto-suggestion. From a happy-go-lucky sort of chap and a good student up to a certain point, he became a failure. He had graduated in fast company and occasionally drunk more than was good for him, and among other things he had learned " to use the needle " to relieve his nerves and conscience after some of his bouts—at first from choice, but afterwards *because he must.* He realised to his horror—brain-fag, loss of memory, incapacity to study, a fugitive appetite, and restless nights. Bad as these were, they were as nothing to the further discovery—he had contracted a habit which he appeared unable to conquer. I need not detail his sufferings—mental and physical—of which he was aware in his better moments. He became encompassed with shame ; filled with confusion ; and at times contemplated self-destruction. Someone had suggested Hypnotism, and he applied to me. I sent him back to Edinburgh and his studies, putting him on a graduated scale of instructions (by weekly letters), commencing with what I knew he could do, and with the happy result that by Non-comatose Suggestion he cured himself of his degrading vices. At the end of six months he visited Rothesay a bright, happy, and healthy young man. He had learnt his lesson and was able to profit by it. HE HAD DISCOVERED HIMSELF AND WHAT SELF-RELIANCE MEANT. I respectfully submit that this is a good example of what can be done by Auto-suggestion where medicinal treatment fails.

Time and space will not permit further detailed cases. There is a host of diseases which can be cured by Auto-suggestion : pernicious habits, whose name is " Legion "; various functional irregularities ; prepossessions ; insomnia—chronic cases can be cured in a few weeks, and permanently too—an infinite variety of troubles, despondencies, chronic headaches, St Vitus' dance, stammering, melancholia, writer's cramp, nervous deafness and blindness, to name a few which have a physical complexion. Then there are others not less real, which are more subjective in character, and are mental limitations indeed—such as, for example, the fear of some person ; the fear of people looking at one ; the fear of places ; the fear of thunder ; stage-fright, and the numerous phases of fear of self ; *want of confidence in performance of that which one is intellectually aware of ability to accomplish, and hence is afraid to undertake* ; " mental abstraction," commonly known as absent-mindedness ; procrastination ; want of system and order ; defective memory—all of which can be remedied directly and indirectly by Non-comatose Auto-suggestion.

There are cases which cannot be cured—too many. Why ? They have no real desire to be cured. A visitor from Wales, who had come for some guidance, complained to me of a once excellent man " down his way " who had taken to drink, first in littles and then in bouts, and who in consequence had his periods of sinning and repenting. The former periods were, however, on the steady increase. " Why does he not get hypnotism to help him ? " I asked, mentioning the names of two or three medical experts to whom his friend might go. " No! no ! " replied my visitor ; " he is too well pleased with himself "—with the state of intoxication in which he was debased.

There is no cure in a case like this; but in all instances where the person is not pleased with himself and the career of vice in which he is entangled, and makes up his mind to be cured, then he can be. NAY, MORE, HE CAN CURE HIMSELF.

NON-COMATOSE SUGGESTION APPLIED

You have only to think about what you do think. Take an occasional half-hour for the purpose in silence and alone. Then set about thinking aright, to some purpose and worthy end, and you will step by step overcome all difficulties in self, and have the greater Self-reliance and ability to face external trials, tasks, and responsibilities, when they arise. That is something worth striving for, but it is not all; the strength and balance which come from quiet reflection will enable you to seize opportunities when they come and also to deliberately make others. This right thinking with conscious effort is Auto-suggestion. And Auto-suggestion is a process of self-education, which, by *attention, repetition,* and *expectation,* brings new ideas to take the place of old, and the thoughts engendered exhibit themselves in action and in life, as do all thoughts—good or bad. By Auto-suggestion the good takes the place of the bad. WE BECOME WHAT OUR AUTO-SUGGESTIONS MAKE US.

For convenience, Non-comatose Suggestions are given by the conscious, voluntary self, to the subconscious, other or inner self, by

(*a*) Physical actions—mannerisms—and

(*b*) By mental and verbal self-direction or instructions.

NON-COMATOSE PHYSICAL AUTO-SUGGESTION

In a long career as a successful hypnotist, when less was known of these subjects than now, I discovered that by placing my subjects in certain attitudes, these physical postures suggested a new train of mentation or thoughts to them. It was not a great discovery, for it was only carrying into hypnotic practice that which is—unconsciously—a daily occurrence in the lives of all. When I placed a subject with his left arm semi-extended, with fist closed, his right arm across his breast with fist closed, his left foot forward, and his body well balanced on right foot, and his head thrown slightly backwards and to the right, the features soon hardened, the lips became compressed, and there was produced an expression of alertness and defiance and aggression in the face. Yet the same subject, when made to go down on his knees, with his hands placed together upraised before him, with his face slightly turned upwards in the attitude of devotion, the hardening of the features vanished, the face became suffused with the tender and gentle expression of the religious devotee. The whole presenting a picture of sincere devotion and a consciousness of dependence on and faith in the Supreme. In both of these cases the attitudes assumed suggested the thoughts which again expressed themselves in the features, and for the time influenced the life of the subject. A little reflection will show that the frequent repetition of such postures or other attitudes will have their correlative mental effects. We also learn from these experiments that the physical postures not only suggest certain trains of thought to individuals, but they also suggest somewhat similar thoughts to the witnesses. It naturally follows repetition of the attitudes form habits, pugilistic or devotional, as the case may be. We should avoid undesirable attitudes, and imitate those more desirable ones which we witness in others.

Now for practical application. You notice the man of firm and determined character; he walks with a firm tread, shoulders well squared back, and with an erect spine; his eyes are steady, his gaze clear, his lips are closed. His speech is possessed by the grace of reserve. We know he means what he says, and respect him. Why not then suggest the qualities of Firmness, Determination, Courage, and Self-reliance to the subconscious self, by making a practice to walk upright,

17

with chest out, shoulders set back, stomach in, lips closed, with eyes steady and to the front? If you have to look at people, do so squarely, although not obtrusively, when addressing them. If you contrast the attitudes of the Self-reliant man with that of the humble and dependent man, you will notice the Self-reliant man straightens every muscle of his body, while the feeble and dependent man goes about with his muscles relaxed. The erect posture with the shoulders squared and well thrown back, and stomach drawn in, is the attitude of Self-reliance. The reverse attitude that of dependence and want of self-reliance. Cultivate then the attitudes of Self-reliance, and in due time you will be Self-reliant.

You will notice that a kindly, courteous person smiles pleasantly; is not a loud-voiced talker; does not rush you with his opinions and arguments in season and out of season; that he "suffers fools gladly"—at any rate, with tact and patience. To his reserve and genial smile, there is the kindly hand. When he shakes hands, there is no flabby, hasty, indifferent grip about it, but a pleasant, attractive hand-shake. Personal Magnetism is the art of pleasing. Every movement shows the graceful and tactful man. Why not suggest these qualities to your subconscious self, by wearing a pleasant smile, by being a good and patient listener, by having a kindly manner, and a more or less hearty, firm hand-grip for those you meet. The practice will do you good. It will become automatic. The shadows from your own mind will pass away; you will find yourself more hopeful and cheerful, less indifferent to the sadness, woes—real or imaginary—of those about you, and your optimism will be helpful to others and yourself.

You will notice that an orderly man is neat in his appearance. He is well-groomed. His desk, his work, and all about him suggest method, order, and taste. He also is able to get through more work because of these things. Why not take a little more care with your toilet, the neatness and appearance of your clothes, the order of your desk, and the arrangement of your papers? Thus, while you are creating a good impression on others, you are by these acts—every one an Auto-suggestion—training yourself in self-respect, order, smartness, and aptitude. The writing of a letter may become Auto-suggestions of care, neatness, thoroughness, and promptitude to one's involuntary powers. All these things will tell in the development of Self-reliance, in business, in success, and in the effects—favourable effects—produced on others.

You will have probably met the individual who at table sups his soup with a noise, shovels his food into his mouth with his knife, drinks his coffee out of the saucer, picks his teeth with his finger or a toothpick, cleans his nails with his pocket-knife, and between these little peculiarities talks mostly about himself, his business capacity, shrewdness, 'cuteness, and his social exploits. You know he is a vulgar person, whether he travels for perfumes or "jungle stuff." He may get on in a way, but his vulgarity and self-assurance would repel persons of taste and culture. Such a man cannot think right and *telepathically influence people before* he approaches them. He is merely a loud-mouthed "drummer," and a coarse specimen at that. His mannerisms and attitudes are suggestions to you of what to avoid. Loud manners and aggressive self-assurance in a traveller may suit some businesses and some employers, but such a traveller is incapable of doing a first-class business or of approaching the heads of really good business concerns.

You will have noticed some men, esteemed well-educated and very capable persons in their own business or professional spheres, and who would be very indignant with the cad-like signs—outward and visible—of the above self-assertive commercial traveller's want of inward and sensible grace, but they are unaware of the defects in their own manners. They are cold, indifferent, and assume a sort-of-lofty-intellectual-superiority-of-the-look-down-on-me order. They manage—consciously or otherwise—to make those about them uncomfortable, and although they do not say much, their attitudes and postures indicate superciliousness, and that they are ever ready to find fault, to be censorious and finicky. Their "exaggerated ego" is a little bit too pronounced, and repellent rather than graceful.

Both extremes are to be avoided, whether at table, in the counting-house, " up country," or anywhere else. Avoid the postures, and you will avoid the attitude of mind which induces them. Assume a virtue, although you possess it not, and it will become yours through adoption. Without effusiveness, be genial. Let your manner show you are at ease ; exhibit urbanity, tact, and "pass the salt" with a cordial smile. Comport yourself with regard to the comfort of others ; your acceptance, refusal, or the offer of a dish or a titbit to others, can be made to enhance the happiness of those about you. Many a decent man has picked a bone with his teeth and eaten his peas with a knife, but there is no necessity for you to do either of these things and give offence. Grace, courtesy—a moderate share of ordinary politeness—cost nothing, and yet on the low plane of £, s. d. are valuable assets.

There are times when a positive and determined attitude is necessary—for there are people who mistake courtesy or good manners for softness, and are short-sightedly ready to impose ; times when a decided "No" or "Yes" signifies a definite conclusion. But there no need to talk about the "mailed fist," or show the "iron hand," till the right time comes—even then let your "Yea" be "Yea" and your "Nay" be "Nay." Never drive when you can draw. IN NINE CASES OUT OF TEN, WHEN YOU MAKE UP YOUR MIND WHOM YOU ARE GOING TO INFLUENCE, AND WHAT YOU ARE TO LEAD THEM TO DO, YOU WILL ACCOMPLISH THAT RIGHT ENOUGH. YOU CANNOT PRACTISE SELF-DEVELOPMENT ON THE LINES OF THESE LESSONS, WITHOUT GAINING MORE SUCCESS THAN FORMERLY.

Thought expresses itself in action. Study the attitudes which are most becoming manliness, character, and worth, and assume these, that they become Auto-suggestions of the right kind of thought in yourself, and you will find yourself growing more and more into right thinking grooves. You see the postures or muscular and physical actions of the lolling, the pro-crastinating, wall-supporting "time killer"; the actions of the angry, irritable, and passionate; the movements of the petulant and impatient. Avoid all these. Check the physical attitude, and you will find yourself check-ing the train of thought which has produced it. Such, then, are some of the simple methods—physical, Non-Comatose Auto-suggestions—by which one can most assuredly improve oneself.

The great secret of the power of Auto-suggestion lies in the fact that all thought is revealed in action. The student of cerebral psychology is aware that the bulk of these actions are unconsciously produced, and are all the more invaluable indications of our mentation. On the stage, the village maiden lightly trips, her steps are short and quick; the villain stalks and strides; the man of thought proceeds with well-regu-lated and orderly steps; the angry man goes stamping about; the lover sighs and moves gently along; the sensualist ogles and leers, and the impertinent fool stares. Quick thoughts and agitated thoughts produce rapid and agitated movements. Quiet, firm, and de-cided thoughts announce themselves in corresponding manners. But this must suffice.

Let us agree that thought ever manifests itself in physical expression. What we become, successes or rank failures, is determined by our thinking. If we desire to be men worthy of the name, we will train, drill, and discipline; we will whip, goad, and lead ourselves to success. All this is best done by deliberate thinking in the secret recesses of our being. The world has nothing to do with this, but it has with our actions. It is not the man who shouts " I am a success ; I know what is best," is either the one or knows the other. Yet even he is better than the man who is always groaning " I am a failure ; ill-luck touches everything I touch." The man who lays himself out in his soul and conscience to prune, fashion, and develop himself in manhood, Self-reliance, and all which that means, will—by steady perseverance—achieve great things ; *i.e.*

First.—The conquest of self, with the power to deny oneself of that which is either injurious or hinders progress.

Second.—The making or the filling of a suitable and reputable sphere of action, with its rewards.

Third.—The respect, confidence, trust, and when necessary, the control of one's fellows.

Fourth.—The attraction to oneself of friends, business, influence, means, and all that manhood, reliability, or character ever wins. The world is wanting and ever ready to pay for men of this type. It is waiting for you.

Auto-suggestion is a process of thinking, done with a definite object, and in a definite way, of which a few examples will now be given in addition to those which have been suggested for practice already. It is not possible to give examples of the phases which are used as vehicles of thought, as employed in Auto-suggestion. But should there be any difficulty in the treatment of self, beyond what is given in these lessons, you are invited to write to me. I will consider the matter and do what I can to help you to help yourself. In my next and last lesson some examples will be given of directly applied Auto-suggestion.

Having quietly pondered over the foregoing, you will not have any difficulty in understanding the meaning of Suggestion and Auto-suggestion. This done, put the Auto-suggestions into practice. Think them, repeat them, practise them, and live up to them.

ATTENTION: Concentrate the mind on a simple, clear suggestion, such as, for example, " I am well ! " or " I am cheerful ! " or " I am self-reliant ! "

REPETITION: Think, dwell on the thought, repeat it mentally—and, when convenient, vocally—till it is familiarly fixed as a convincing thought.

EXPECTATION : This is the philosophical synonym for Faith. You look for the fulfilment of the thought, which you have incorporated in self, by attention and repetition. Your expectation is sustained by the knowledge that all thought, conscious and unconscious, manifests in action, translates itself into flesh and blood: what you truly think—auto-suggest—you are. You expect to become healthy, cheerful, and self-reliant, because you have put yourself in the way of these things. Sincere thought fulfils itself.

PRACTICE: You affirm Health, Cheerfulness, Self-reliance, by Auto-suggestion procedure; that is, you practise in thought, and, as far as lies in your power, you honestly endeavour to live up to your thought. You practise again what you think.   You become what you think.

In this glorious gospel of healthy egotism, Self-help, you find that ATTENTION, REPETITION, EXPECTATION, and PRACTICE are the mighty levers of the mind by which you raise yourself to the performance of whatever is noble, honest, straight, and true, and upon which you have fixed your mental eye and aspire to accomplish.

YOU BECOME WHAT YOU HAVE DESIRED TO BE.

YOU ARE WHAT YOUR REPEATED THOUGHTS AND ACTIONS HAVE MADE YOU.

SUGGESTION RULES THE WORLD, AND YOU HOLD THE KEY.

CHAPTER XVI

NON-COMATOSE AUTO-SUGGESTION (*continued*)— MENTAL MODES

"We are all sculptors and painters, and our material is our flesh and blood and bones. Any nobleness begins at once to refine a man's features, any meanness or sensuality imbrutes them."—THOREAU.

IN bringing these lessons to a close, it will be as well to once more remind you of the reciprocal interaction of mind and body. Whatever may be the mental trouble—from mere impatience, anger, or sleeplessness, to undesirable states of lack of mental co-ordination or intellectual self-control—it is certain, whether one is aware of the fact or not, to be preceded by some state of ill-health in brain or body. Before proceeding with Auto-suggestion in connection with that defect, it is advisable to see that attention be paid to the laws of physical health. Let everything done in the matter of breathing exercises, in drinking, eating, and rest, be made optimistic Auto-suggestions of Health. Before long there will be a physiological adjustment of function, corresponding to the demands of the mind, and in the correct employment of the foregoing physical

266

agents greater harmony—health—of mind and body will be induced.

In my experience of Auto-suggestion treatment, I find mental defects are as amenable to cure as bodily diseases. The cures are not so much a matter of faith or expectancy as a conscious realisation of improvement from the steady perseverance in the use of the means. The mind is developed, and the body controlled by the conscious exercise of Non-Comatose Suggestions. I respectfully maintain that Therapeutic Suggestion lies at the basis of all these cures, and that whatever hypnotism, Christian science, mental science, faith-healing—within and without the churches—can accomplish, as the reward of faith, you, who read these pages, can—with or without faith—accomplish for yourself. You can and are ever educating your own mind; your mind acts on your body; your body becomes a reflex of your mind. Your thoughts become actions. AS YOU THINK, YOU ARE. THAT IS TRUE. NOTHING CAN BE TRUER. YOUR THINKING IS, AS YOUR AUTO-SUGGESTION MAKES IT. CHANGE YOUR AUTO-SUGGESTIONS AND YOU CHANGE, REMAKE, YOURSELF. You have been doing this all along. Have courage, and proceed as in previous lessons, but with a fuller process:—

1. Write out your Auto-suggestions to remedy the particular defect you desire to overcome. Let your suggestions be simple, to the point, and they will be more effective in consequence.

2. Arrange with yourself for at least three periods daily—of about a quarter of an hour each—for privacy,

and to give yourself the suggestions. In a word, take your mental medicine three times daily.

3. When you retire, put yourself into an appropriate state of receptivity. First on waking in the morning and when going to sleep at night, you will be in that state naturally. At other periods it can be induced.

4. After you have given yourself the suggestions for five minutes or so, pause and think over the attitude of mind you desire to attain; picture its effects on the body as a present possession. Then resume the Auto-suggestions in a simple, earnest, self-convincing and reassuring manner for another five minutes. Lie still for a little, and then rise and dismiss the whole for the time being. Go about your business with renewed cheerfulness, and you will find that you are carrying out your Auto-suggestions, almost unconsciously—naturally.

Please note: all suggestions have to be repeated to become incorporated or fixed in self, as the following will make sufficiently clear. Suppose you are introduced to a gentleman. You shake hands and spend a short time in his company. You meet him again some time afterwards; you remember him perfectly, your conversation and mutual effects, but are annoyed to find you have forgotten the name. It is very awkward. Possibly you reflect, "I have a bad memory"—a very bad Auto-suggestion to make. Your memory is all right, your brain machinery is all right too. What is wrong? Nothing wrong. *The name was mentioned only once in the interview*, but the personality of the man was impressed upon you during a sufficiently long period, by many thousand vibrations of colour, of sound, of feeling, of sensation, and of thought. There was little or no chance to forget the man, but no reasonable chance to remember the name. It was not sufficiently repeated (by yourself) to be remembered.

Auto-suggestions require repetition, interest, and a time period, to become—fixed—part of self. Once incorporated in the subconscious self, the recording centres of the brain, are never forgotten. Therefore Auto-suggestions, accepted in a susceptible state, repeated and thought over, become self. There is no occultism in the matter, unless the processes hidden from actual consciousness be occult. Carry out Non-Comatose Suggestions with interest and repetition, and you will remake yourself. You will do more: you will discover yourself a brighter, better, and more successful man than you knew yourself to be. Correspondents write to me, "Thanks for your lessons; I am a new man." "I am now astonished at my health, vim, will-power, and energy," etc.

Thanks are always grateful, but the secret of the change lies in the change of thought these clients put into their Auto-suggestions. "The hopeless, despondent wreck of two years ago is a practical man of affairs to-day." Auto-suggestion created new lines of thinking; the thoughts created new channels and exhibited in new and better modes of action, in a newer, clearer, and better life.

It would be as impossible as it is unnecessary to

give examples of Non-Comatose Suggestions, suitable to every case. Something must be left to the wit and ingenuity of the man who means to help himself. Two or three guiding hints must suffice:—

Write your Auto-suggestions, and then read them over several times. If need be, cut them down. Make them terse and clear. Think over them, and by thought, graphic, visual, and auditory vibrations, they will become more or less recorded in the cerebral centres before being ground in by voluntary conscious effort. When this is properly done you rise above yourself and direct your own life into proper channels, as a wise, loving, and firm teacher directs the mental and moral steps of a child in whom he is most interested. The more earnest and thorough the Auto-suggestions, the more successful the results in conscious experience.

The next step is to place yourself in a receptive or quiescent state. If not so naturally as in waking or going to sleep, you can always induce it by retiring into solitude. Free yourself from the restraints of clothing; lie level on bed or sofa in a limp or relaxed muscular condition. Close your eyes, keep out the wakeful effects of light, and you will help meditation and concentration thereby. Breathe softly, slowly, and fully. By this procedure your intellectual self will be positive, and yet the rest of your mind will be in a receptive and negative state, sensitive to thought-vibrations given in a definite manner. Proceed to give the suggestions, mentally, verbally, and psychically— by thought, speech, and vision—such as picturing out the state desired. All these modes are practised unconsciously by everybody. But you will do this consciously for present and for anticipated results.

To further help you to put Non-Comatose Auto-suggestion into practice, we will take as illustrations the self-treatment and cure of INSOMNIA and SELF-CONSCIOUSNESS, and also the procedure for increasing SELF-RELIANCE. We will take a case of Insomnia first. We will commence by admitting the disease, and by acknowledging the causes which underlie it are many. We admit all causes—mental and physical —and deny nothing. We will suppose the trouble has reached the chronic state, and that the mental state of the patient is pretty low. He is fitful, procrastinating, peevish, and undeterminate. Can a person in that state cure himself? Yes. Let attention be drawn to and paid to the improvement of physical necessities. By attending to proper breathing, the sufficient employment of liquids, suitable food, and a moderate degree of physical labour, the blood is purified and enriched, and labour suggests desire for rest, sleep.[1]

---

[1] The majority of persons suffering from insomnia sit and brood over their troubles with the tenacity of a brooding hen hatching out chicks, and unintentionally exaggerate the trouble of which they complain and which a little more physical exertion would do much to remedy.

INSOMNIA

SUPPOSE that you are the patient. Make up your mind to sleep at night, and you will sleep. To help you to make up your mind, use Auto - suggestions. Should sleep be slow in coming owing to anxieties during the day or something which has excited and upset you during the evening, and about which you may be peevish and worrying, drop it all, and set your mind to get sleep and fix on *the idea of sleep.* Relax the body; close the eyes, and breathe softly and slowly—with just enough conscious effort to be aware that you are doing so. After two or three minutes of this, tell yourself mentally — while inhaling :—

"SLEEP, SLEEP, SLEEP, SOUNDLY, SOUNDLY SLEEP."

While retaining the breath :—

"I AM SLEEPY, HEAVY WITH SLEEP, SLEEPY."

While *slowly* EXHALING :—

"I AM PASSING INTO SLEEP; SLEEPING SOUNDLY, SOUNDLY SLEEPING."

During the brief interval before inhaling again :—

"SLEEP, SLEEPING, ASLEEP, SLEEP. SLEEPING."

As you breathe so softly and slowly, repeat the foregoing some ten or twelve times in the order here given ; the idea of sleep will become more fixed. The words are simple, the intellectual effort is not great, and the changes rung on the word SLEEP will :—

(*a*) Reduce your mental activity, excitement, and worry to the lowest point. At moments you will forget them.

(*b*) You are accustoming your thoughts by concentration, gradually but surely, to the idea of sleep, and by inhibition of mental activity in other directions producing sleep.

RE-ENFORCEMENT BY PHYSICAL MODES

Suppose you have repeated the respirations with the Auto-suggestions for twenty times, and still sleep is fickle to be wooed. Keep the body relaxed, and curl up comfortably on your side ; turn the eyeballs slightly upwards, still keeping your eyes closed, and proceed steadily with the suggestions as before. The posture and the thoughts will keep the mind on sleep and sleep conditions, and you will assuredly sleep. A whole night's sleep may not be achieved at first; but look forward to it, and it will come. In waking moments do not worry about sleep, but quietly resume the soft breathing, and keep on suggesting sleep to yourself, as outlined. By breathing, posture, mentation, repetition, and concentrated attention on SLEEP, SLEEPING SOUNDLY, you are inducing sleep.

ANTICIPATORY SUGGESTIONS

In the morning, before rising, a more ambitious effort should be made—something after this style. For a short time lie quietly and easily. Think of the comfort and happiness which sound sleep brings; then relax the body and resume the quiescent, receptive state, and proceed as follows :—

"TO-DAY I AM MORE ACTIVE AND ENERGETIC; I WILL SLEEP WELL TO-NIGHT."

Never mind the breathing methods, but give yourself this double suggestion in this way. Once, mentally; twice, whispered; three times, uttered in convincing semitones; and once in ordinary voice—the whole emphatically. Then the last half, " I WILL SLEEP WELL TO-NIGHT," in the foregoing fashion.

"TO-NIGHT I WILL SLEEP BETTER; I WILL SLEEP SOUNDLY AND WELL. I WILL SLEEP SOUNDLY."

Give yourself this suggestion in the manner already adopted, with the exception that you will repeat it several times in full, and finish off with :—

"NOW I WILL DO BETTER TO-DAY, AND I WILL SLEEP WELL TO-NIGHT."

Rise, promptly dress, and don't go moping about—find something useful to do.

In the afternoon, find a suitable spot for a quarter of an hour's retirement, and devote it to the anticipatory suggestion that you will sleep to-night.

"TO-NIGHT I WILL SLEEP BETTER. I WILL SLEEP SOUNDLY; SLEEP SOUNDLY AND WELL."

When you have done this half a dozen times in the manner already pointed out, pause and adjust yourself in the most inviting attitude of sleep, and again repeat the suggestion. Yawn two or three times and repeat the suggestion in a drowsy, easy manner. Rest for a little; then get up and find something to do.

Taking for granted, then, that you are a victim of Insomnia, do not be foolish enough to exaggerate that state—as some do—by declaring, during the day, to your friends and others, "Oh, I slept very badly last night"—"I am such a poor sleeper"—"I try hard, but I can't get sleep." This unhealthy fishing for sympathy will not help you. Avoid the topic, and keep quietly persuading yourself: "I WILL SLEEP WELL TO-NIGHT" as being the wiser course of procedure. NO WEAKNESS. Make up your mind that YOU WILL SLEEP, AND SLEEP YOU WILL.

In the evening, avoid all exciting subjects. Do not talk about yourself, nor take your state too seriously. Indulge in pleasant conversation; and at night if you think a hot foot-bath, or a warm trifle in your stomach, such as a tumblerful of warm or hot milk, will help you to sleep, then have them by all means. Go to bed and deliberately lay yourself out for sleep: for sleep thoughts, sleep talks to self, and sleep attitudes. Proceed as you did on the previous night and the great probability is, that before you are half-through, you will inhibit all active thinking and pass into the land of dreams.

Suppose you are not a victim of Insomnia—well, avoid it by keeping before your mind's eye: "IT IS BETTER TO SLEEP THAN TO THINK IN BED."

SELF-CONSCIOUSNESS

AUTO-SUGGESTIONS FOR NERVOUS TIMIDITY, SHYNESS,
WANT OF CONFIDENCE, BACKWARDNESS, ETC.

NERVOUS timidity, want of confidence, is very amenable to non-comatose Auto-suggestion, and the results are astonishing—in a few months timidity, bashfulness, shyness, nervousness, and associated want of faith in self become things of the past. The treatment can be carried out before rising and after retiring for the night, and sometime during the day. Suitable Auto-suggestions should be written out. The following procedure will serve to illustrate :—

"I AM A MAN, MANLY; I AM NOT AFRAID. THERE IS NOTHING TO BE AFRAID OF."

Three times mentally—three times whispered—four times uttered in semitones—four times in the natural voice—once aloud and emphatically.

"IT IS EXCEEDINGLY FOOLISH TO BE TIMID. I AM A MAN, MANLY. I ACT WORTHY OF MY MANHOOD."

Give these suggestions to Self in a similar manner to the above.

"I AM MANLY; I AM NOT AFRAID. I AM NO LONGER TIMID; I AM A MAN, MANLY. I AM A MAN."

Now proceed as before.   Remember the importance
of repetition and its ultimate effect: the creation of
a stronger and more desirable habit.

MENTAL RE-ENFORCEMENT

Pause; sit quietly and picture yourself a man, level-
headed,   reserved,   and   strong.   Imagine   you   are
confident.   Think over what you want to do.   Is it to
see someone you would rather not see? to read an
essay, "speak a piece," face an authority or the public?
—Whatever it is, think it well over and see yourself
coolly facing it:—

"I AM COURAGEOUS. I AM NO LONGER TIMID.

"I AM COURAGEOUS, BOLD, RESOLUTE.

"THERE IS NOTHING TO BE FEARFUL ABOUT.

"I WILL DO IT. I WILL DO IT WELL. YES, I WILL
DO IT."

There are several allied suggestions here.   Dwell well
on each, and with calm conviction repeat in somewhat the same order as before.   Then imagine that you
have risen up and are standing chest out and head
erect, and feet firmly placed, and assure yourself with
mental, verbal, and physical Auto-suggestions:—

"I AM NO LONGER TIMID. I AM FEARLESS. I AM A
MAN, MANLY.

"I AM A MAN, READY AND ABLE TO DO ALL THAT
A MAN CAN DO.

"I DO NOT FEAR. I AM COURAGEOUS"; and conclude the exercise, which is carried out as before, by

repeating six times the last Auto-suggestion, with clear and definite emphasis :—

"I DO NOT FEAR! I AM COURAGEOUS!"

The Auto-suggestions can be added to and varied to suit special cases. They can also be enhanced by actual physical postures, elsewhere called "RE-ENFORCE-MENT BY PHYSICAL MODES."

During the day, in field, workshop, office, or on horse-back—fix the mind on the simple phrases : "I DO NOT FEAR! I AM COURAGEOUS!" Think them, whisper them, say them, and in a little time you will act them. You will be what your thoughts are. You will be astonished at your own powers, your courage and fearlessness. And this will not be all. You will discover that you have made decided physical improve-ment : digestion, sleep, energy, pose — all greatly improved, and promising further improvement. Your manly straightforwardness, your wholesome, decided "Yes" or "No," will be refreshing and convincing. Your language and actions will be those of a man who does not fear and is courageous.

SELF-RELIANCE

IT does not follow, although health is a factor in Self-reliance, that the want of the latter is a sign of ill-health; but as a foundation of all mental improvement, force of character, will-power, it is advisable to convince yourself of physical health and vitality, and let this, like a golden thread, run through all *your mental exercises of which Auto-suggestion is the Most Practicable.*

Three times mentally—	"I am healthy, buoyant, and vigorous."
Three times whispered—	"I am healthy and vigorous."
Three times in semitone—	"I am healthy and Self-reliant."
Three times in semitone—	"I am healthy, vigorous, and Self-reliant."
Once aloud with emphasis—	"I am vigorous and Self-reliant."

280

Suggestions of Self-Esteem to follow.

Three times mentally—	"I am independent, self-confident, and dignified."
Three times whispered—	"I am self-confident and not afraid of responsibility."
Three times in semitone—	"I am dignified and maintain my Self-respect. I cannot do a low thing."

Once aloud—   „   „

Repeat these suggestions in the above order three times, slowly, convincingly, and thoroughly.

Three times mentally—	"I am self-confident. It is right to be manly and Self-reliant."
Three times whispered—	"I am manly and Self-reliant. I do not hesitate. I use my own judgment."
Repeat—	"I am manly and use my own judgment."

Once aloud—   „   „

You will do well to repeat the foregoing three times in the order given, and this last suggestion also, three times—

"I am manly, decided, and use my own judgment."

SELF-ASSURED RE-ENFORCEMENT BY MENTAL VISION

That is best done by dwelling for a few moments on the vigour and joy of health. The good of it all, and your own determination to make life worth living —as far as the exercise of your own judgment in matters of health is concerned. Place your hands kindly on the cheek bones, and assure yourself, " I am well, happy, and strong." And think what it is to be so to the best of your ability. Then see yourself, walk in a Self-reliant, self‑confident, and determined manner, as one determined to take your own advice and act upon it. Whatever the consequence, you will act as you have decided on, knowing that you will do nothing unworthy of a MAN— YOURSELF.

Suggestions of Firmness to follow.

Three times mentally—	" I am firm and decided. I have a strong will."
Three times whispered—	" I am persevering, resolute, firm, and decided."
Three times in semitone—	" I am resolute and decided. What I take in hand, I carry through."
Three times in semitone— Once aloud—	" I CAN and I WILL accomplish what I take in hand."

| Three times whispered—
Once aloud with emphasis— | "Stability and fixedness of purpose mark the man. I AM STABLE, FIRM, RESOLUTE." |

Give these suggestions to self in this order: once mentally, three times whispered, three times in semitone and once aloud.

Suggestions of Courage to follow.

Three times mentally—	"I am courageous, manly, and resolute."
Three times whispered—	"What is worth doing, is worth doing well. I am courageous. What is right, I do."
Also three times whispered—	
Also three times in semitone—	"I am courageous. WHAT IS RIGHT, I DO."
Once aloud—	

MENTAL VISION, RE-ENFORCEMENT OF HEALTH, SELF-ESTEEM, FIRMNESS, AND COURAGE AUTO-SUGGESTIONS

Think of the advantageous aid it would be to self in public life to speak what is on your mind for the best. How you have been crippled from fear of some defect in delivery, or of some person or from criticism! Remember that no man is either infallible or perfect, whatever he may become; but the Manly Man does his best—true courage comes from sincerity, sincere and firm convictions. In future you are not going to bother yourself about your appearance or the form of words in which you shall express yourself; in the discharge of private or public duties you will say and do that which you are convinced and believe to be right. You see yourself standing up boldly, without the fear of man, and speaking in a courageous spirit. You fear no foe and shrink from no encounter, and see yourself, in public as well as in your private life—plucky, bold, resolute, and vigorous. Whatsoever your hands find to do, that you do, with all your might. A cringing, apologising, please-think-well-of-me spirit is far from you, and you see yourself, a Self-reliant, energetic, resolute, and courageous man.

Dwell on the man who looms up in your mind as the healthiest example of Faith in Self. There are countless leaders in political, religious, commercial life, and in Art, Science, Medicine, and Philosophy, from whom you can easily pick some man, who, by the cultivation of Self-reliance, and with little or no help from his fellows, has achieved wonders. These are the silent, strong men who have made history, and made their country great; have built Orphanages, and accomplished many other great things—have risen from very small beginnings. What they have done in their sphere, you see yourself doing in yours. You can be a silent, strong man too, and by Faith, in the powers of your being—known and unknown—may see yourself, a MAN MAKING THE BEST OF YOURSELF AND OPPOR-

TUNITIES, for you are not holding back from what you should do from lack OF COURAGE or WANT OF FAITH IN YOURSELF.

Please note that it is not intended that the Formula for Self-reliance is to be carried out at one time. The HEALTH and SELF-ESTEEM suggestions in the morning; the SELF-CONFIDENT and MANLY suggestions in the afternoon; and the suggestions of FIRMNESS, with full MENTAL VISION, RE-ENFORCEMENT, can be given to yourself at night. These properly given will bring about a marked improvement in character, ability, and pose in due course.

Test the foregoing thoroughly. Give at least fifteen minutes three times a day to them. Commence as you mean to finish. Have no anxiety about results. What you aim at will be yours right enough.

As to practical re-enforcement of all Suggestions— LIVE UP TO THEM. This you will find yourself doing as a rule. But in some cases, at the outset, you may find yourself tested. Don't give up and back out, when you should do neither one nor the other. You will be better of this victory over yourself, and stronger, braver, more determined and Self-reliant when the next public test comes. Have the courage of your convictions. Leave " hedging " to gamblers. Don't " hedge " to keep square with politicians, party, churchmen or laymen, to hold position or post. Quietly pursue your own way, and the joy of minding your own business, family affairs, and convictions, and you will find the progress gained in Self-reliance by these means a treasure of happiness without price, and a tower of strength and a place of true safety within, which will make life truly worth living.

The foregoing examples for practising Auto-suggestion in Insomnia, Self-consciousness, and Self-reliance, may or may not suit your particular case, which may be laziness, or that of over-work; selfishness, want of order, lack of concentration, or some other defect; but as you are an intelligent man and mean to help yourself and keep your end up, whatever happens in the field, you will make up your own special formula to suit your special case.

You can convert many phrases in this volume into Auto-suggestions. Build yourself up cheerfully. Get hold of right, good, helpful, sound, vigorous thoughts. The world is brimful of examples. Coin healthy, moral, and spiritual suggestions out of them. Tell yourself—

"I feel better now. I am improving all the time. The breathing exercises have done wonders for me. I feel better and brighter and more alert. Work is a pleasure. I can concentrate now. Trifles do not upset me. 1 succeed. I mean to succeed. Nothing less than the best will satisfy me.

"This drink improves my digestion; it increases all natural secretions, and improves my digestion. My food agrees with me. The breathing exercises, the liquid, and care in the mastication of food purifies my blood, and perfects all natural functions.

"I am healthy, active, and clear-headed. I am gaining in VIM and energy daily. Every breath I breathe, every sip of water, every mouthful of food, does me good. My food, my work, my rest, and my sleep—all make for sound, virile health.

"I am becoming, I am growing stronger daily. I am healthy and strong. I am resolute, persevering, and clear-minded. I am more resolute, cheerful, and energetic to-day. I am stronger, better, and brighter every day.

"It is good to be alive. I am alive, and will make the most of my life. To-day is mine, I will use it for the best.

"I am healthy and strong, vigorous and resolute. I am courageous and fit. I feel fit for . . . task. I do not shirk responsibilities. I can do it, and I will. I will, and I can, and I will do it. Do it now.

"I am Self-reliant, determined, ambitious, and energetic. I am Self-reliant, determined, and aggressive. I am not afraid of opposition. Failure does not daunt me. I can and I will overcome. Repulsed to-day, I win to-morrow. That which I believe to be right I do. I succeed all the time. Patience, plod, and good-nature tell all the time.

"I am Self-reliant, magnetic and attractive. My patience and cheerfulness draw people to me. My thoughts and actions are magnetic. I influence and attract friends. I attract business. My manner begets confidence.

"I am considerate to the young. I love their

buoyant, bright spirits, their unspoilt confidence and trust. I respect and esteem the old; their age, experience, sufferings, and feebleness, demand cheerful and thoughtful attention.

"I am benevolent, kindly, and cheerful. By kindly, cheerful smile and pleasant manners I will show a gentle and cheerful disposition.

"I think of the good within all. I am not disposed to judge. When I do not know, I will think the best. I try to make others happy. My manner affects others for good.

"I will not judge hastily. I put myself in his place. Yes, I might have done the same. It is best to think lovingly and kindly of all.

"I will wrong no man. I deal straight. 'Goods according to sample' is my motto. My word is as good as a bond. Men shall trust me. I will be trusted.

"My manners are good. I am patient and considerate. My thoughtfulness, cheerfulness, and industry bring me friends, influence, and success.

"I want to do what is best. I am doing my best. Nothing less than the best will do. I am thorough, energetic. I believe in working when work has to be done. There is a time for all things.

"I am very decided. I am firm. If I have to choose between dogged determination and brilliancy, I place my faith on the former to pull me through. I am determined and firm.

"I am determined, firm, resolute, persevering, energetic, and magnetic. I am becoming more and more magnetic every day. I have a quiet, positive, and magnetic influence over my fellows.

"I value doing one thing at a time. My success is due to that. I am successful. I am a success. Quiet, steady perseverance overcomes all difficulties.

"I am successful. I am a success. I put my best into what I do. I succeed because I sleep, rise, think, work, and live to succeed. A useful, energetic life is its own reward. Better do little things well. One step at a time is the way of success. That is my way.

"My life is useful. It brings happiness, love, confidence, and success. I am successful, because I have determined to be so." And so on.

"I am neat and orderly; I dress well. First impressions are important. It is good for my self-respect; on business and civil grounds—first impressions are important.

"I live my best life; guard my lips. I watch my manners; and I go ahead. I live my best to-day. My life makes for happiness and success. I tackle difficulties first. I am improving daily. I know I am. I will not fail. Initiated? No. I control myself. I succeed. I am a success.

"I command success. I am successful. I succeed. My employer is pleased. I make up my mind to please. I succeed. I am a success.

"My men (or manager or man) are (or is) doing better. *My thoughts* influence them for good. My actions influence them for good. I am determined to get their best. They will serve me right. I draw them. I succeed.

"I mean to influence . . . He will come round and see as I do. He knows I have his interests at heart. In serving me, he advances his own interests. I do what is right. He will come in. I will make him feel. I watch him, and justly reward. I get his best."

Terribly egotistic all this! Perhaps so. But remember that you are drilling yourself, and you will be as you drill, but DO NOT SAY THESE THINGS TO OTHER PEOPLE, NOT EVEN TO YOUR DEAREST FRIENDS. YOU WILL BE TO THEM AND YOURSELF AS YOUR ACTIONS PROVE YOU REALLY THINK YOU ARE. YOU WILL BE AS YOU THINK. Think health and you will be healthy. Think Self-reliance and you will be Self-reliant. This is no wild assertion; it is a sober truth founded not upon personal observation alone, but by comparing the notes of many just and keen observers. You want to be as Self-reliant in public as you feel you are in private. You do not feel Self-reliant in public, are hampered in expression because you are self-conscious, *i.e.* think and expect to be so. Well, by proper Auto-suggestion you are drilling yourself, not to think so, but to think something else, *and you will become as you think.* Never mind what you imagine other people will think about this or that or about yourself—perhaps you are too anxious on that score. BUT DO MIND WHAT YOU THINK YOURSELF; FOR WHAT YOU REALLY THINK YOU BECOME AND ARE.

You desire to improve in a certain direction; start making Auto-suggestion to that end, and you will soon really think as you have suggested, and that means you really will have become as you have learned, and disciplined yourself to think. YOU CAN PROVE THIS IN YOUR OWN CASE by carrying out this mental treatment effectually.

THE AUTO-SUGGESTION OF YESTERDAY BECOMES THE THOUGHT OF TO-DAY.

THE THOUGHT OF TO-DAY BECOMES THE MAINSPRING OF ACTION.

REPEATED THOUGHTS AND ACTIONS BECOME HABIT, PART OF YOURSELF.

IN FACT THAT WHICH YOU FREQUENTLY SUGGEST TO YOURSELF, YOU BECOME.

TELEPATHY AND SUCCESS

Now just a word or two in conclusion. Self-discipline and improved Self-reliance have enabled you to think straight and control yourself, and to draw others to you, with advantage to both them and yourself. This has demonstrated to you the power of Auto-suggestion, and in a measure the power of mind over mind. You have realised by directing your own mind; by the repeated thinking of right thoughts, the very vibrations of thought have stimulated and strengthened your brain and improved the physical conditions or health of the body. You are now ready to learn to influence others by the action of your mind on others. You have learned to do a great amount of good and useful work without speaking, or only speaking when courtesy and sound judgment suggest the necessity. But you have not thought it possible to prepare others for your approach, and to lead them to favourably approve or accept your ideas, by fixing your thoughts upon them in advance. This can be done and is done daily. Minds are influenced; diseases are cured by mental actions of the patient or client whose mind is directed thereto by some other mind, *en distance*.[1] Call this Telepathy, or by any other name—it is a fact. Why not apply this power of the mind to favourably influence and direct other minds? It can be done, and done successfully, just in proportion as we succeed in controlling and directing self.

It is true we can only influence those who are more or less *en rapport* with ourselves. But it is impossible to know who is and who is not without experimenting. Then, again, there may be sympathy on one plane and not on another. Anyway, telepathy is an undoubted fact. It is more; it is an undoubted factor in a magnetic, successful life. My recent work, *Seeing the Invisible*, will help you to understand something more of the finer forces and powers of the mind. Our unspoken thoughts influence our fellows for good or evil, and so this power of the mind has been used for good and evil in all ages. To think evil and plot selfishly with regard to others is to work our own ruin;

---

[1] This is called by practitioners of Suggestion, ABSENT TREATMENT. Many are helped to CURE by this process, who have not confidence at first to go in fully for Self-treatment.

impure, vile thoughts debase body and mind—soul, if you will. But the deliberate, conscientious exercise of thought, employed in the influencing of others, not only is a definite and possible, but a powerful factor in all friendship; in social life, between husband and wife, between correspondents and in business relations.

The manner of achieving success, through subconscious channels, is similar to that of Non-Comatose Suggestions. Retire into privacy. Instead of placing the body in a relaxed state, take a normal attitude, either sitting or walking. Bring the individual to be influenced before your mental vision. Put yourself in his place. Bring your best thoughts to bear on him. Think the thoughts you would like him to think. Weigh well in your own mind what you want to attain. Is it a matter of approaching interview, of correspondence, of friendship or business—think it out for him. Don't dictate; that arouses antagonism. Don't say—

" You must pay me that sum.

" You must see me or you must come to me."

Put yourself in his shoes, as it were, and think for him.

" I really must pay that account. I will make an effort to do so.

" I will arrange to pay and let him know when I can.

" I will not postpone the matter longer. I will see Mr . . . (yourself)."

After this fashion send out your thoughts briefly and

definitely. Dwell on the thoughts as on an Auto-suggestion, which he—the person influenced—is giving himself. Be masonic, and yet more than a mason. The free and enlightened masonic brother will reveal his secrets to an approved and tested brother. *You keep yours to yourself.* You will quietly, definitely, and repeatedly concentrate your mind on the message you desire to be entertained. In the majority of cases you will create a favourable impression. That is worth the trouble. The practice will enable you to equip yourself more fully to break down obstacles, subdue antagonisms, and to handle difficulties in your life work. Try it. Keep your own counsel and you will succeed. One success begets another. Nothing succeeds like success. Patient and steady application tells in this as in all other things.

I cannot advance more at present, but I can assure you, if you have faithfully carried out my previous instructions, you will be able to prove the success of these suggestions. You will soon be able to gain the trust and confidence of those near and dear to you. You will draw to yourself religious, political, and business connections by exercising what is now called "Telepathy." There is nothing occult about it. The mother employs it when thinking or praying about her boys or boy ; the lover of his absent fiancée ; friend when thinking of friend; the dying of the living, and the living of the—so-called—dead. All I suggest is that you employ your thoughts to influence the living in a practical and definite way. You have learned how to influence yourself for good. You will be still doing so, by thinking healthy, bright, and sensible thoughts for others. Both methods are best, and the whole procedure makes life more worth living, and develops true Self-reliance, and all that is comprehended in the term.

FINIS

Index

BY THE SAME AUTHOR

SEEING THE INVISIBLE. Practical Studies in Psychometry, Thought Transference, Telepathy, and Allied Phenomena, with 5 plates. Crown 8vo, cloth, 5s. net. Post free 5s. 4d.

"SEEING THE INVISIBLE," ACCEPTED BY THE KING.

The Author has been honoured by the following letter from Buckingham Palace, dated 6th December 1906 :—

"The Private Secretary is commanded by the King to thank Dr Coates for his letter of the 3rd inst., with the accompanying copy of his book 'Seeing the Invisible.'"

"A deeply interesting work of 300 pages, dealing with Man's Psychical Nature, Invisible Forces and Emanations; Nature's Invisible Biograph; Psychometric Experiments and Practice; Thought-Transference and Telepathy; Psychic Faculty, Telepathy, and Modern Spiritualism."—*Two Worlds.*

"Among the many volumes that are issued from the press on the all-embracing subject of Psychology . . . . none has yet appeared of such a practical and interesting character as the volume bearing the above title, by James Coates, Ph.D., F.A.S."—*Harbinger of Light*, Melbourne, Australia.

"A distinct acquisition to the literature dealing with psychic faculties." —*Light.*

HUMAN MAGNETISM: OR, HOW TO HYPNOTISE. With 10 plates. Fourth edition. Crown 8vo, cloth, 5s. net. Post free 5s. 4d.

This is an excellent work by a master of the subject. Mr Coates is no mere theorist, but has had a long practical experience of the subject with which he deals so ably. In the introduction to the work he gives a short sketch of the progress of the science from the earliest times.

THE PRACTICAL HYPNOTIST. Concise Instruction on Hypnotism. The Art and Practice of Suggestion in the Cure of Disease, the Correction of Habits, Development of Will-Power and Self-Culture. With 2 Plates. Fcap. 8vo, cloth, 1s. net. Post free 1s. 2d.

Hypnotism has come to stay, and ere long its non-employment will be esteemed little less than a criminal neglect, where patients are not amenable to medicinal substances. . . . There are thousands who are invalids to-day who can be helped to help themselves, by the way of Auto-Suggestion or "New Thought Powers," to Health of both body and mind.

"HOW-TO" MANUALS

HOW TO READ HEADS. 128 pp. Illustrated. Bound in Boards. Price 1s., post free 1s. 2d.

HOW TO READ FACES. Copiously Illustrated. 128 pp. Boards. Price 1s., post free 1s. 2d.

HOW TO MESMERISE. HOW TO THOUGHT-READ. 128 pp. Illustrated. Boards. Price 1s., post free 1s. 2d.

IMPORTANT TO CORRESPONDENTS

Readers of the above published works, desiring Professional Advice or Instruction in connection with matters dealt therein, should send all letters —with stamped and addressed envelopes—direct to author at his private address, "Glenbeg House, Rothesay, Scotland," and not to Publishers. By this procedure, unnecessary delay in getting replies will be avoided.

www.ingramcontent.com/pod-product-compliance
Lightning Source LLC
Chambersburg PA
CBHW062117020426
42335CB00013B/995